Send

Send

The How, Why, When
– And When Not –
Of Email

DAVID SHIPLEY

and

WILL SCHWALBE

CANONGATE

Edinburgh · New York · Melbourne

First published in the USA in 2007 by Alfred A. Knopf,
a division of Random House Inc., New York

First published in Great Britain in 2007 by Canongate Books Ltd,
14 High Street, Edinburgh EH1 1TE

1

British Library Cataloguing-in-Publication Data
A catalogue record for this book is available on
request from the British Library

ISBN 978 1 84195 994 8

Printed and bound by GGP Media, GmbH, Poessneck, Germany

www.canongate.net

WS:

For David Cheng

And Mary Anne and Douglas Schwalbe

In Memory of David Baer and Robert H. Chapman

DS:

For Rosa and Joseph

And Joan and John

CONTENTS

Send

Why Do We Email So Badly?

Bad things can happen on email.

Consider Jo Moore, the Labour Party press officer and special advisor to the Department of Transport, who committed the following thought to email on September 11, 2001:

From: Jo Moore
To: Alun Evans; Mortimer, Robin
Date: 11/09/01 14:55:12
Subject: Media Handling

Alun
It's now a very good day to get out anything we want to bury. Councillors expenses?
Jo

CC: Corry, Dan

The email was sent to the Department's director of communications and another top civil servant, and copied to a policy advisor. Ms Moore resigned shortly afterwards.

Or consider us.

Once upon a time, we were trying to figure out when we needed to get a draft of this book to our editor, whom we'll call Marty. (After all, that's his name.) No problem, right? We were (reputedly) literate professionals—Will, the editor in chief of a publishing house, and David, the editor of *The New York Times* Op-Ed page—setting a basic timetable. It wasn't contentious. It wasn't emotional. It wasn't even all that complicated.

Here's how it started:

Marty sent us an email—Subject line: "One for the book?"—about an angry email he had written and regretted sending.

Why was Marty sending us this note?

David took the email at face value, assuming that Marty had simply wanted to pass along an anecdote for us to include. Will, however, suspected that this was Marty's gentle way of eliciting a status report.

If David was right, the correct response would be simply to thank Marty for his contribution and leave it at that. If Will was right, the proper reply would be to email Marty a detailed memo, giving him a date by which to expect the manuscript.

David answered promptly, following his instincts. (He copied Will.)

Subject: One for the book?
To: Marty
From: Shipley
Cc: Schwalbe

Dear Marty:
Thanks for the anecdote. This will fit right in.
All best,
David

Will started to formulate a progress report, but then, before he had finished it . . .

Marty sent another email. In this one, he wrote how helpful it would be to have a portion of the manuscript to show his colleagues at an upcoming meeting.

OK, this time we both agreed his note was a pretty unmistakable request for us to send him part of the book. The problem: we weren't quite ready. So we needed to figure out whether getting him part of the book was "helpful" or "essential." David thought the former; Will thought the latter. Regardless of who was right, the ball was now in our court. So what did we do? We began to panic and behave like lunatics.

First, we did the worst possible thing: nothing. Days went by. Perhaps the email would just go away. Then we wrote a convoluted response—one that reflected our eagerness to buy ourselves as much time as possible to finish the manuscript but that was also meant to reassure our editor.

Here it is:

Subject: One for the book?
To: Marty
From: Shipley, Schwalbe

Dear Marty:
Thanks so much for yours. The writing is going well, but we're not quite there yet. We really want to get you something for your upcoming meeting, but we're not totally sure we can do it in time. We're wondering how much of the manuscript you need and the last date we can get it to you. Is there a part of the manuscript that you're particularly interested in having? We have a complete first draft, but some parts are more polished than others. Perhaps we can talk next week so that we can let you know where we're at and discuss how to proceed.
All best,
Will and David

And here's Marty's reply:

Subject: One for the book?
To: Shipley, Schwalbe
From: Marty

I'm going on vacation next week. Let's talk when I return.

Ouch. Clearly, Marty was fed up with us.

Or not ouch? Was he?

Was he throwing up his hands and saying, "Whatever. I'm going on vacation"? Or was he simply saying, "This is a complicated topic. I can't talk about it right now because I'm leaving on vacation. I'll talk to you about it when I get back"?

By the time we had sorted out our timetable, three weeks had passed, lots of emails had been exchanged, and a question that should have taken one minute to answer had eaten up hours. We had come face-to-face with one of email's stealthiest characteristics: its ability to simulate forward motion. As Bob Geldof, the humanitarian rock musician, said, email is dangerous because it gives us "a feeling of action"—even when nothing is happening.

So what is it about email? Why do we send so many electronic messages that we never should have written? Why do things spin out of control so quickly? Why don't people remember that email leaves an indelible electronic record? Why do we forget to compose our messages carefully so that people will know what we want without having to guess? We wrote this book to figure out why email has such a tendency to go awry—and to learn for ourselves how to email not just adequately but also well. Our Holy Grail: email that is so effective that it cuts down on email.

We don't hate email; we love it. We recognize that email has changed our lives in countless good ways. We just want to do it better. In fact, we think it's kind of remarkable that people manage on email as well as they do. After all, the odds are against us.

For starters, email hasn't been around all that long. Search for the term "email" in *The New York Times* archive for the mid-1980s and you're as likely to turn up "Thomas E. Mails" (author of *The Pueblo Children of the Earth Mother*) as you are references to electronic communication. It wasn't just that email was rarely used—it had barely been invented; before 1971, the @ sign was used mostly by accountants and merchants. There was no official Internet before 1983. America Online (AOL) did not become a household name in the U.S. until 1989.

That's a far cry from where we are today. Trillions of emails are sent every week. Office workers in the U.S. spend at least 25 per cent of the day on email and countless hours on their handhelds. In 2009, the Bush administration is expected to turn over more than 100 million electronic messages to the National Archives. (The Clinton administration, by contrast, left behind 32 million emails in 2001.) All the data shows that email usage is continuing to grow.

A more detailed history of email lies ahead. The point we want to underscore here, however, is that this new technology took over our world in about a decade. Just as previous generations struggled to integrate first the telegraph and then the telephone into their lives, we're struggling to integrate email into ours. We're using it and overusing it and misusing it. Email is afflicted by the curse of the new.

Still, our difficulties with email can't simply be blamed on its youth. They also stem from email's unique character—or lack thereof.

If you don't consciously insert tone into an email, a kind of universal default tone won't automatically be conveyed. Instead, the message written without regard to tone becomes a blank screen onto which the reader projects his own fears, prejudices, and anxieties.

"Will you be late for the meeting?" is a simple question. But simply stated in an email, it can give rise to a huge variety of reactions. An employee who is on probation could see this as a stern warning. A model employee could interpret this as an insult, thinking, "I'm always on time, why would he now think I would show up late?" Or it could provoke confusion: "Why would I be late for the meeting? Is there something going on beforehand that I should know about?"

Email demands, then, that we figure out who we are in relation to the person we're writing to and that we get our tone right from the outset—but this isn't as straightforward as it sounds. As poet Walt Whitman reminded us, we contain multitudes. We are bosses and employees, mothers and daughters and sisters, scolders and comforters, encouragers and discouragers—and we constantly blend and change roles, even when we're talking to the same person.

Yes, all written communication is harder in this respect than interactions that take place in person, or even over the telephone: you cannot revise your message according to the reactions you're getting from the other party as you proceed. But email is the hardest written medium of all.

Letters, at least, give us clues that can help us divine their meaning. Personal stationery says something different from corporate, and gives hints as to what is inside. As linguist Naomi Baron has noted, whenever we write a letter, we know we will be judged against centuries' worth of expectations. We remember that letters are permanent and so tend to use our best spelling and grammar.

Even other forms of electronic communication trip us up less frequently than email. Instant messaging and texting come close to replicating the real-time back-and-forth exchange we associate with in-person conversation—and they tend to take place (IM *always*) among people with whom you have some sort of association or affinity. They have a relatively consistent default tone—one of chatty casualness.

Email offers no such salvation because we email both for informal communication (making plans with friends, asking questions of peers) and for formal communication (applying for a job, pitching a prospective client). The distinctions get blurred, sometimes to dangerous effect.

We also email fast—inevitably too fast. We are in the position of having to get our messages right dozens or even hundreds of times a day, often under intense pressure, and for recipients whose needs, attitudes, and moods are constantly changing.

To complicate matters, the speed of email doesn't just make it easier to lose our cool—it actually eggs us on. On email, people aren't quite themselves: they are angrier, less sympathetic, less aware, more easily wounded, even more gossipy and duplicitous. Email has a tendency to encourage the lesser angels of our nature.

There's a reason for this. In a face-to-face (or voice-to-voice) conversation, our emotional brains are constantly monitoring the reactions of the person to whom we're speaking. We discern what they like and what they don't like.

Email, by contrast, doesn't provide a speedy real-time channel for feedback. Yet the technology somehow lulls us into thinking that such a channel exists. As Daniel Goleman, author of *Social Intelligence,* told us, emailing puts people, in neurological terms, in a state of disinhibition. (In our non-scientific terms, it's cluelessness.) When we're on email, the inhibiting circuits in our brain—which help us monitor and adapt to our audience's responses—have checked out.

The big problem, of course, is that we aren't always aware of this. And by the time we are? Well, we've probably already hit that Send key.

Like Jo Moore, we've said incredibly stupid things on email.

And like, well, us, we've used email to dither.

We've also emailed badly because we were too quick on the draw. We've emailed badly because we've forgotten who we were in relation to the person we were writing to, or because we pushed the wrong key; not inserted enough personality, or shared a little too much of our inner, emotional selves. (If you are in receipt of, or receive, a really terrible or thoughtless email from either Will Schwalbe or David Shipley—and we know our names are attached to plenty of them, alas—please accept our apologies.)

Email has vastly increased the amount of writing expected of us all, including people whose jobs never used to require writing skills. As a result, we all complain about the sheer quantity of emails we receive, but what's often overwhelming—and overlooked—is the *quality* of the messages we exchange.

Sure, there exists a gap between those who came of age

before email and those who came of age after it emerged—between those who know how to manage the technology but often don't know how to write appropriately, and those who know how to write but don't know how to use the technology at their disposal. But no age group has a monopoly on bad or good emails.

So what can we do to email better? In the pages ahead, we'll show you how (with a little mindfulness and a few simple rules) we can all avoid email disasters and begin to use this powerful communication tool to get what we want—both at work and in our personal lives.

To: The Reader
From: Shipley and Schwalbe
Subject: The First Chapter—When Should We Email?

Let's get started.

The Eight Deadly Sins of Email

1. The email that's unbelievably vague. ("Remember to do that thing.")

2. The email that insults you so badly you have to get up from your desk. ("HOW CAN YOU NOT HAVE DONE THAT THING?!!!!")

3. The email that puts you in jail. ("Please tell them that I asked you to sell that thing when it hit $70.")

4. The email that's cowardly. ("Here's the thing: you're being let go.")

5. The email that won't go away. (Re: Re: Re: Re: Re: Re: Re: that thing.)

6. The email that's so sarcastic you have to get up from your desk. ("Smooth move on that thing. Really smooth.")

7. The email that's too casual. ("Hiya! Any word on that admissions thing?")

8. The email that's inappropriate. ("Want to come to my hotel room to discuss that thing?")

CHAPTER 1

When Should We Email?

Would you carry a violin in a damp knapsack? Would you wrap your fiancée's birthday present in used cheesecloth? Would you mail your grandmother's stemware in a paper bag?

How you send something can have a profound impact on *what* you're sending. Your method of delivery sends a message of its own.

Here's the verbatim text of an electronic message sent to the phone of a young woman who worked for a hip fashion store in Wales:

> We've reviewed your sales figures and they are not really up to the level we need. As a result, we will not require your services anymore. Thank you for your time with us.

There's a trend here. Radio Shack did the same thing recently. After a series of meetings about impending layoffs, about four hundred employees were told by email that they were being fired.

The work force reduction notification is currently in progress. Unfortunately your position is one that has been eliminated.

Nice. We need to remind ourselves that just because we have email, we shouldn't use it for everything. Because of the speed and the seeming urgency of the new forms of communication available to us, many people simply grab the closest thing at hand. Or they get lured into eye-for-an-eye exchanges: if they get an email, they reply by email; if they get a letter, they feel compelled to respond by letter. We can do better than that. It's really a matter of taking the time to consider the strengths and weaknesses of each form of communication before committing to one.

That said, figuring out what medium is right for what message can be confusing. Today there are more ways to communicate than ever before. When should you email? And when is a text message more effective? How about a letter, or picking up the phone? (You remember those?) Or even a personal visit?

Or—and this seems to be one of the most effective and least used options—simply doing nothing at all.

Match Game

Take one item from each column. Which of these go together? Try to mix and match:

Email	Boss	Casual	Request
Text	Friend	Urgent	Solicitation
Mail	Colleague	Routine	Thank-you
Phone	Assistant	Unexpected	Critique
Fax	Mentor	Emotional	Apology

It's not clear-cut, is it? Do you text a friend a routine thank-you? Or do you phone? Do you fax a colleague an unexpected critique? Or will email work for all of the above? To find your way to the best decision, you need to understand the communication technologies at your disposal. Let's start with the strengths and weaknesses of the one that many of us use the most and understand the least.

Email

Seven Big Reasons to Love Email

1. *Email is the best medium ever created for exchanging essential information.* What time is the movie? Where is the restaurant? Who's coming to the meeting?

Before email, any one of these questions would have involved at minimum a call, often to someone who wasn't there, necessitating a message (possibly garbled by a third party on one of those awful pink message slips). The return call might meet a similar fate.

And say your call wasn't one of the 70 per cent that, according to Bill Gates, wind up in voicemail, and that you did manage to connect easily. Etiquette demands that you enter into a far longer exchange than the answer to your question strictly requires. At the very least, you are obligated to engage in several minutes of pleasant but not particularly productive conversation, whether or not you have time to spare.

Email has been blamed for the death of the letter. We think that's unfair. Email is responsible for the death of the useless phone call. (And, by the way, it was the telephone that killed the letter.)

When Will was editor in chief of a publishing house in the early 1990s, he used to receive fifty to sixty phone calls a day—and not one email. Even though he's in the same job now, at a different publishing house, he receives only ten to fifteen calls daily. Much of what used to require a phone call can now be taken care of more efficiently with email.

But as the Cat in the Hat says, "That's not all!"

2. *You can reach almost anyone on email—and not just business people.* Recently, Duncan Watts, a sociologist at Columbia University, updated for email the famous "six degrees of separation" study, which demonstrated that anyone can be connected to any other person through a chain of no more than six acquaintances. Watts asked the people participating in his study to see if they could get an email message to someone they didn't know: "a professor at an Ivy League university, an archival inspector in Estonia, a technology consultant in India, a policeman in Australia, and a veterinarian in the

Norwegian Army." The catch was that you could forward a message only to someone you knew. The forwarded messages that hit their targets did so after an average of only four connections.

Another clear benefit: You can get your message to a list of a half-dozen or one thousand people as easily and inexpensively as you can get it to one person. And most email addresses can be easily found or sleuthed.

3. *Email knows no time zones—it's an efficient and economical way to communicate with people around the world.* You can also write an email any time of the day or night and have it sent the minute it's finished—or, if you are moderately clever, program it to be sent hours, or even days, later.

4. *Email gives you a searchable record.* Even if you do make an efficient phone call, there's no record of it. Are you going to trust the other person's "notes"?

5. *Email allows you to craft your message—or your response—on your terms and on your own schedule.* Unlike a conversation, email gives you time to think about what you want to say.

6. *You have the choice of preserving and presenting parts or all of a string of pre-existing emails.* This enables you to refer to what came before, to bring newcomers up to date, or, without anyone knowing, to delete irrelevant or inappropriate parts of the correspondence.

7. *Email lets you attach and include additional information that the recipient can retrieve when and if he chooses.* This means instant access to maps, supporting documents, photographs, charts, spreadsheets, links, and so on.

A Brief History of Email, for Anyone Who Cares

In the early 1960s in the U.S., the Pentagon decided that it needed to be able to harness the power of all its computers more quickly. (To respond to things like, oh, Soviet missile launches.) So it asked its research arm—the Defense Department's Advanced Research Projects Agency, or DARPA—to build the world's first computer network. The project, called ARPANET, connected UCLA to Stanford on October 29, 1969. The first message sent over this network was "LO"— although it would have been "LOGIN" if the computer hadn't crashed.

The world's first email—a small message between two ARPANET computers—was sent a couple of years later, in 1971. By this time, each user of an ARPANET computer had a rudimentary "mailbox." Ray Tomlinson, a computer scientist in Cambridge, Massachusetts, devised a simple address for messages sent from one user to another, using the user's account and the computer's name, separated by an @. As Tomlinson remembers it, the first message he sent was gibberish; the computers were in the same room, and Tomlinson was both the sender and receiver, so he didn't bother with a sentimental or grand historic declaration.

Initially, ARPANET's physical network consisted of a few long-range connections between the East and the West Coasts. But it grew, and in 1983 the network was split into military and civilian branches. (The military's branch was renamed MILNET; we civilians were given ARPANET.)

By the time it sprang free, ARPANET wasn't the only civilian network around. Research groups and organizations in the civilian world had started to establish computer networks of their own. These networks would soon merge with ARPANET to form the early Internet.

For that integration to take place, however, computers in these different networks needed to be able to talk to each other. They needed a simple, efficient protocol for sending information. Enter TCP/IP, which had been created in 1974 but wasn't adopted by ARPANET and other networks until New Year's Day, 1983. Now, almost a quarter of a century later, TCP/IP is still the standard protocol of the Internet. IP (or Internet Protocol) deals with addresses while TCP (Transmission Control Protocol) regulates the way messages are divided up and sent.

Once the rules were in place, competing services started popping up everywhere, as telecom companies entered the fray. In 1983, MCI introduced MCI Mail, which charged subscribers forty-five cents to send a 500-character message. (This came with a special feature: MCI would call users to tell them they had received electronic mail.) CompuServe jumped in the game, as did America Online, which (wisely and lucratively) positioned itself as the service for people who were uncomfortable with, or new to, computers. Lotus, Microsoft, and others introduced products that made it simple for businesses to use email companywide. Suddenly, email wasn't so scary anymore. The rest is history.

Eight Reasons You May Not Want to Email

Email's strengths are also its weaknesses. We're going to explore these at some length—not because we're negative guys but because you can't be certain that email is the appropriate mode for a message until you've considered all of its limitations and dangers.

1. *The ease of email encourages unnecessary exchanges.* Because it's so easy to engage in brief exchanges on email, people email way too often. They ask questions when they don't really need the answers (or when they could have found the answer another way). They also send information that doesn't need to be sent and extend conversations long past their expiration date.

That's not to say we're against *all* unnecessary exchanges. A casual encounter, whether in person or on email, can cement a social bond and sometimes even lead you to information that proves useful later.

Rule: If you wouldn't stop by a colleague's office every ten minutes for a chat, you probably don't want to email him frivolously thirty times a day.

2. *Email has largely replaced the phone call, but not every phone call should be replaced.* Because email is at a physical and temporal remove, it can be an awkward tool for reaching agreement, finding common ground, or bringing things to a close.

Rule: Conveying an emotion, handling a delicate situation, testing the waters—all these challenges are usually better undertaken with the human voice.

3. *You can reach everyone, but everyone can reach you.* The world of email appears hierarchy-free. Many people who were once out of reach are now, theoretically, within grasp. Many CEOs read their emails unscreened—whereas an unfamiliar, inappropriate letter isn't likely to get past an assistant. We all get plenty of emails every day from people we've never met—people to whom we have never given our private email addresses—simply because these individuals have found their way to our personal inboxes by some not-so-hard-to-divine combination of first initials, last name, and corporate address . . . or just by searching the Internet.

This flatness has its egalitarian appeal, but it's also a source of genuine confusion because it fosters a lack of formality that's often misguided. If you were a new employee in, say, tech support, you wouldn't dream of walking into the CEO's office with a minor complaint. If you were a student, you wouldn't think of calling your professor in the middle of the night with a question about an assignment you didn't understand because you were hungover in class. And if you were going to make a presentation in a foreign place, you'd learn about local etiquette and rules first—and not simply barge into a conference room in, say, Dubai or Seoul.

Email is both so intimate and so easy that it makes unwise actions far more likely: once you have someone's address, you can contact that person any time of the day or night from your very own office or bedroom. This once unimaginable access clouds our ability to discern who we are in relation to the person we're writing to. Consequently, people issue wildly inappropriate requests to their correspondents that can damage their relationships and derail their careers.

Some of the most telling conversations we've had are with professors and college admissions officers, who have seen the once-respectful divide that used to separate them from students and applicants evaporate with email.

David Haig, a head tutor in biology at Harvard, regularly gets emails from students he's never met that are addressed "Hey, Professor Haig," or "Hiya." And Bill Fitzsimmons, dean of admissions at the university, tells us that he now receives long, slangy, and sometimes sloppy emails from applicants. While he made clear that these messages don't cause a student to be rejected out of hand, they do at times make him question the judgment of the writer, especially if there are other concerns. "Ever since email came on the scene," he said, "there are people who have thought, wrongly, that there are different rules with regard to familiarity—that all bets are off because it is a different medium."

The students sending these emails seem painfully unaware that the person they are writing to (and annoying) is the same person who could be offering them a place in a freshman class or grading them at term's end.

A related problem is how to separate the *genuinely* familiar from the *overly* familiar. The Subject line or the sender's name can sometimes indicate which messages you'll want to read right away, which can wait, and which ones will aggravate you. But they aren't foolproof. And even programs with preview panes, which show you the message before you actually open it, only save you one click. You still have to read the thing.

For people fortunate enough to have assistants, email presents another problem. So much email is confidential that many companies prohibit executives from letting others access their email accounts. Busy people are left with the choice of sorting through an enormous inbox every day or of breaking the rules and entrusting their privacy (not to mention the power to send emails under their name) to someone else. After the World Economic Summit in Davos in 2006, a participant reported that one of the most hotly debated issues among global leaders was this: Should you allow support staff to manage your inbox?

A 2002 online poll conducted by the International Association of Administrative Professionals and the ePolicy Institute found that 43 per cent of administrative assistants write and send emails under their boss's name; 29 per cent are allowed to delete emails before their boss has seen them.

Here's what Bill Gates does. He has software that cuts his email intake from thousands of emails a day to about a hundred by letting through only those messages that come from people with whom he has corresponded in the past. The rest go to assistants who then sort and summarize them.

> Rule: When it comes to outgoing messages, don't assume instant familiarity. And when it comes to incoming ones, try filters. But keep in mind that current filters are usually imprecise or overly restrictive. Until smarter filters come along, you should think twice before giving out your address.

4. *The fact that email defies time zones also means that it can defy propriety.* It can arrive when you're trying to finish a project, when you least want another task. As Clive Thompson pointed out in *The New York Times Magazine,* you often don't know if an email is worth opening until you open it; opening it takes time and attention; the interruption can eat away at productivity. After a worker has been interrupted with a message, it generally takes nearly half an hour for him to return to his original task. And that's assuming he *returns* to that original task. According to researchers cited by Thompson, 40 per cent of workers moved on to completely new tasks after they were interrupted, leaving their old task behind, neglected and unfinished.

> Rule: Don't forget that every email is an interruption. If the matter isn't urgent, a letter can be less intrusive.

5. *The fact that email always provides a searchable record means that you can be held accountable for your electronic correspondence.* Not only everything you've sent but also everything you've received can come back to bite you. (More on this in Chapter 6 when we discuss the legal implications of email.) There are two types of office creature who take advantage of this. For the person who delights in saying, "I told you so," email is the most satisfying invention in history: he can throw your own words back in your face. Email is also a great way to pass the buck, and for the person whose primary instinct is to cover his own backside, email provides endless opportunity to expose yours. How many of us have received messages that bury, amid chatty and barely relevant detail, one informational time bomb. (For example, "the shipment may be late" . . . "looks like we might be over budget" . . . "just wanted to let you know that the bank called.") But when the bomb goes off, it will be your fault. After all, there's proof you were told and given plenty of notice to act. There's an email record to prove it.

> Rule: If you're working with weasels, watch their emails like a hawk.

6. *The ease with which an email can be forwarded poses a danger.* Keep in mind that your message can also be sent on to people for whom it was not intended. Sure, this could be done via mail. Someone could photocopy a letter that puts you in a bad light and mail it to mutual acquaintances, but he or she would look almost as bad as you—the effort required

highlights the malice behind the action, whereas the ease of email camouflages it, somehow.

Rule: Never forward anything without permission, and assume everything you write will be forwarded.

7. *With email, your words can be changed.* Forwarded emails can be invisibly edited or altered—and without your knowledge if you've been cut out of the chain. (Jack Abramoff, the powerful Washington lobbyist with Republican Party ties, who pleaded guilty to fraud in 2006, wrote with glee about forwarding email messages that he'd "played with" in order to "scare" clients into doing what he wanted them to do.) Even if your forwarded email is left untouched, its context and meaning can morph if the message to which you were responding is altered or omitted.

Rule: If you need to send a sensitive document via email, one where it's essential that your words not be messed with, send your message in a .pdf (see page 85) or some other hard-to-alter attachment.

8. *Email attachments don't just come with baggage—they are baggage.* They harbor viruses. And they take up valuable server and computer space. If someone sends you a message with one hundred .jpegs (see page 86), it can fill up all the space you've been allotted on a corporate server, and prevent you from sending or receiving new emails until you delete that message—something you may not be able to do if you're out of the office and on a handheld.

A warning about attached Word documents: they may include Track Changes (a program that shows previous edits). If you don't want people to see the history of what's been done to the document, make sure the changes are accepted and purged. Otherwise, embarrassment may ensue. An "independent" business leader who was set to offer testimony to Congress was found, via Track Changes, to have allowed a Bush administration official to edit his statement. As the unmasked man told the *Los Angeles Times,* "The real scandal here is that after 15 years of using Microsoft Word, I don't know how to turn off 'Track Changes.' "

(To really turn the darn thing off, click on the Track Changes button on the Reviewing toolbar, or press Ctrl+Shift+E and de-select "Highlight changes." Then email it to yourself and see if you can find old edits. If not, go ahead and send. And hope for the best.)

Rule: Before you send an email laden with attachments, keep in mind the following: pack carefully and travel light.

A Quick Word about the Handheld

We know by now that email doesn't just come to your desk. We are also finding out that the BlackBerry and its cousins can be demanding and addictive in a way that desktop email isn't. They can turn employees into serfs, on call 24/7. And the temptation to check email (or the requirement that you do so) can mean that you are never free from the demands of work.

Because thumb-typing leads people to be less literate and more abrupt, it's not always the best choice for sending a message, though choosing to keep the tagline "Sent from handheld" may encourage people to forgive you your trespasses. And the limitations of email—that it's not good for complex or emotional messages—are even more pronounced when you are composing or reading messages on a handheld's tiny screen.

WRITERLY APOLOGIES FOR HANDHELD STYLE

Sent wirelessly via handheld, so pardon the terseness and typos.

—Harlan Coben, novelist

Typing with my thumbs on handheld.

—Richard Dooling, novelist

People are forgiving of handheld typos—and with good reason. A study in a 2006 issue of *Psychological Science* looked at the decrease in reading speed associated with different types of misspellings. When letters are transposed in the middle of words containing five or more letters, there is only an 11 per cent drop in reading speed. When the transposition is at the beginning or the end of words, the drop is 36 per cent and 26 per cent, respectively. Which means midword typos—the kind you usually see in handheld messages—are no more than a minor inconvenience.

To wit, try to read the following spurious email, which is currently enjoying an active life on the Internet:

Aoccdrnig to a rscheearch at Cmabrigde Uinervtisy, it deosn't mttaer in waht oredr the ltteers in a wrod are, the olny iprmoetnt tihng is taht the frist and lsat ltteer be at the rghit pclae. The rset can be a toatl mses and you can sitll raed it wouthit porbelm. Tihs is bcuseae the huamn mnid deos not raed ervey lteter by istlef, but the wrod as a wlohe.

Handheld technology is not great yet at handling some attachments and very large documents. Therefore, an important courtesy to observe when sending an attachment to someone you suspect might be on a handheld is to provide a summary of what the attachment includes and the urgency (or lack thereof) with which the recipient needs to review it. A good Subject line, one in which the first few words describe the message, is particularly helpful.

There are three main types of handhelds—those that automatically get new emails "pushed" onto the screen as soon as they are received anywhere (that's the Research in Motion/BlackBerry technology), those that pull emails in on a schedule (every ten minutes, say), and those that make you fetch your messages. The first two are quicker and more efficient; the third, which requires a bit more effort, is better for recovering addicts who are trying to get out of the habit of checking their inboxes every ten seconds or so.

Much has been written about handheld etiquette (about people who check during dinner, on vacation, at a concert, in a meeting, at the park with their kids). All we have to add is this: handheld checking is not all that different from any other sort of behavior that demonstrates you aren't paying full attention to the people you're with. Our suggestion: ask those around you to tell you if your handheld use (addiction? obsession?) is bugging them. If in doubt, cut it out.

How Does Email Work?

The Internet is the network of nodes (mainly servers, routers, and switches) that connects computers. The Internet carries data, including the World Wide Web, instant messaging, and email. The data travel between nodes in many different ways: via fiber-optic cables, wireless signals, copper wire, or satellite and radio connections.

When you hit Send on your email program, your message is carved up into packets. These are individually labeled with the recipient's address and with the part of the message that the packet contains (e.g., "bytes 1 to 500").

The address—or domain name—is structured hierarchically, like a postal address. Read the address, starting from the end, and you'll find the most general division of the Internet, the top-level domain: *.com, .uk, .edu, .gov,* and so on. The top-level domain is preceded by the name of the organization, and the name of the router that serves a particular department or division. Domain names correspond to numerical addresses, for example, 123.28.102.35. Each number in the address can have a value between 0 and 255.

The routers communicate using the numerical address.

Simple Mail Transfer Protocol, or SMTP, is the protocol that governs the communication of addresses between servers. If the message being sent contains only text, SMTP also handles the transfer of the text of the message.

Multipurpose Internet Mail Extensions, or MIME, is a more advanced form of email, set up to deal with messages that SMTP can't transmit, like those that do not use standard characters, symbols, and numbers. MIME also handles attachments. Nearly all email and Webmail programs use both of these formats to send messages across the Internet.

For most of us, email systems come in three flavors: local mail, hosted mail, and Webmail. A local mail server (also called a Local Area Network mail server, or LAN mail) consists of a server at your organization that handles email only for the organization. Hosted mail works the same way—except that the server is housed off-site by a provider like AOL. To the email user, these two systems appear nearly identical. Webmail may be a component of local and hosted servers, and it is also the system used by Hotmail (soon to be renamed Live Mail) and Yahoo.

POP (Post Office Protocol) and IMAP (Internet Message Access Protocol) are the two primary ways of organizing local and hosted mail servers. Users sometimes have a choice of which protocol their email client will use. POP servers can be configured so that once you "pick up" your messages from the server (by clicking Check Mail on your program), the messages are stored either on your computer or on both the mail server and on your computer.

IMAP is a newer protocol that stores all messages on the server. It is mainly used by large organizations. Messages on IMAP servers arrive a little faster than on POP servers, and there are ways to download IMAP messages to your computer, but IMAP is most useful in situations where users are always connected to the server. Most individuals still use POP.

Email Alternatives

Just because we have email doesn't mean that we should use it for everything. There are plenty of other forms of communication to which you can turn. Here's when to deploy them and why.

The Letter

In a 2006 study, 1,400 office workers were asked about their correspondence habits. Though three-quarters of those surveyed said that they couldn't live without email, fully a third reported that they still sent letters and faxes every day. This isn't just epistolary nostalgia. The letter simply possesses some practical virtues that you won't find in email.

Letters aren't interruptions. We can walk into the mailroom at work when we want, pull out the letters jammed in the mailbox, and open them—when we feel like it.

By looking at the envelope, the return address, the handwriting, and the stamp, we can often get a sense of whether it's something we need to open quickly or not. We also know that someone had to go out of his or her way to send a letter. The value of a letter—be it a thank-you note or an apology or a condolence—easily exceeds that of even the most effusive or abject email. A handwritten note makes it personal; a typewritten letter on company stationery makes it official. Each in its own way comes with a weight that email will never have.

We like letters most of all because we can change our mind about whether we want to send them. As far as the world knows, the letter doesn't exist until it goes in the mailbox. (Word to the wise, however: once a letter *does* go into the mailbox, attempts to retrieve it may subject you to federal prosecution.)

The letter has withstood just about every technological assault. Though Abraham Lincoln was so entranced with the telegraph that he would spend hours in the White House telegraph office reading the electronic dispatches from the front, he knew when only a letter could do the job. As Tom Wheeler writes in *Mr. Lincoln's T-Mails: The Untold Story of How Abraham Lincoln Used the Telegraph to Win the Civil War,* Lincoln could have dashed off a telegram of congratulations to General Grant [upon the capture of Vicksburg]. Instead, he picked up a pen and wrote a gracious and humble letter that concluded, "I now wish to make the personal acknowledgment that you were right, and I was wrong." It was a message made all the more powerful by the fact that it was from Lincoln's pen directly to his general's hand and not transcribed by a telegraph clerk.

Six Reasons to Send a Letter Instead of an Email

1. When you want a document that can be filed (in a cabinet), archived (paper can last for centuries; no one knows about the durability of electronic archives), or framed.

2. When you want to create something that the recipient can savor, like a letter of commendation or a love letter.

3. When you don't want to interrupt someone.

4. When you want to present and address complex topics.

5. When you really mean business: a registered letter, a subpoena, a memo stating company policy.

6. When your material is so confidential that you can't take any chances it might, with a mere click of the Forward command, find its way to someone other than the intended recipient.

The Fax

Many people wrongly predicted that email would kill the fax machine. Email was the asteroid; the fax was the dinosaur. Even pioneering Hewlett-Packard got out of the fax business thinking that it had no future, only to return a few years later when the technology proved resilient.

As of this writing, fax machine sales are hanging in there. That doesn't mean that faxing occurs indiscriminately, as it did when the machines hit critical mass. It means that people and businesses have figured out precisely what faxes should be used for.

Three Reasons to Send a Fax Instead of an Email

1. Because a fax can come with what is considered a true copy of an actual signature—and can therefore be legally binding in many instances. This means you can do something that you can't easily do with a plain email: sign a contract or exchange signatures to close a deal. The law is in flux over when emails can be used to accept the terms of an agreement, especially if all the parties haven't agreed in advance that an email will suffice.

2. Because you can send important hard documents—a contract, a schematic, a child's drawing—rapidly. If you want to email the thing, you

have to scan it into your computer, and by the time you do that you could have faxed it.

3. Because it's more secure. Once loaded onto email, a document can easily be sent anywhere and everywhere. That's less likely to happen if you're faxing one copy to one recipient—*although you do need to remember that fax machines are often public.* We both share machines with others and are therefore often guilty of glancing at (OK, reading) faxes in the inbox that weren't intended for us. Faxes are also not infrequently picked up unintentionally with other faxes, thereby getting mislaid for indefinite periods of time or lost. That is why it is always good to alert the recipient that a fax is on the way and to retrieve an expected fax from the machine as quickly as possible.

And remember, some programs and commercial services allow you to transmit an email so that it emerges from someone else's fax machine, or to receive as an email a document originally sent by fax.

The Telephone

We don't think of ourselves as old, but we recall when the phone was a big deal. We grew up with rotary dial and clicking units of time. To waste minutes talking about the weather or what you were going to wear to school was to invite a scolding. And you couldn't always call when you wanted to. Will remembers waiting hours one evening in London in the seventies for an operator to call back with an available overseas line. In the eighties, David kept Sunday nights for his once-a-week call to his parents on the other side of the country.

Even though we now take clear and easy phone communication for granted, it's still possible to find pleasure—and a little bit of that old-time feeling—chatting with someone on the phone. There is something intimate about a phone call. Unlike an email, a phone call is live. You interact in real time. It's the difference between a play and a movie. (True, cell-phone quality can still be aggravating, but it's a lot better than it was, and reception is improving all the time.)

Try an experiment. Call a friend and say, "I'm mad at you" in a tone that conveys that you aren't—the tone you would use if the next sentence was something like, "You didn't tell me about your promotion." Then ask your friend if she thought you were truly angry. The answer will probably be no. Now imagine what would have happened if you had sent that pal an *email* that read, "I'm mad at you."

Our voice is a very subtle instrument and can convey not just cartoon emotions (Fury! Misery! Joy!) but every shade and nuance in between.

Robin Mamlet, former dean of admissions at Stanford and now an executive recruiter, never uses email to check references. Her reasoning? When she's on the phone, a pause or a strained voice in response to a question about work habits can sometimes hint at a more complicated answer than the one she's been given. If Mamlet hears hesitation, she can push and maybe get the whole story. An email answer might not have given her the clues she needed to follow up.

Unlike email, the phone gives you the opportunity to change course. If you're on the phone and you sense the conversation going south—maybe that joke *wasn't* so funny, maybe that tactic *wasn't* such a great idea—you have time and space to tack and find a better course.

Just the other day, Will found himself in the early stages of an email war with a colleague. The parties were moving farther and farther apart, more intent on scoring points than on solving problems. When one particularly inflammatory email came back in response, Will set to work composing and recomposing replies, ranging from reasonable to sarcastic to livid to icy. When he saw that an hour had passed, he realized not only that he had wasted a good part of his day but also that none of the responses he'd considered would help bring the matter to a close, not even the very calmest one. The great time saver had morphed into the great time suck. The only hope of resolution was a phone call. Will called and the conflict sorted itself out. It doesn't always turn out this way, of course, but remember that it can.

Why do people use email in cases when they know they should be using the phone ("If only I'd called him . . .")? Maybe it's because the phone can be troublesome—numbers to look up, voicemail hell, the dread of catching someone at a bad moment, chatterboxes. Or maybe it's because when the news is bad, the phone takes courage (unless you take the cowardly route and time your call to get voicemail—a tactic harder to employ now, with the proliferation of cell phones and caller identification). Or maybe some of us take delight in flame wars at the expense of solving the problem at hand. Or maybe it's just easier to live life at a distance. Whatever the reason, there are some things that Alexander Graham Bell's 130-year-old invention still does best.

Seven Reasons to Use the Telephone Instead of Email

1. When you need to convey or discern emotion.
2. When you need to cut through the communication forest. Sixty-seven emails have gone out and you still haven't finalized that meeting? In three phone calls, it's all set. (Date, time, location, roster of participants, who's having what for lunch.)
3. When you need to move fast. (Yes, it's true—even with cell phones, you can have trouble finding someone, or you can get stuck in voicemail. Still, the phone is faster and more reliable than anything else. When you've actually found someone, you know it.)
4. When you want a remote communication to be private. (Unless you're being recorded or speaking really loudly—and rudely!—in a public place.)
5. When you need to reach someone who doesn't have—or doesn't check—email.
6. When you want people to be able to engage and respond immediately. The fact that we can talk at the same time and interrupt each other means that we can communicate the way we do in person. The phone allows our words and ideas to overlap,

mingle, and amplify one another. Instant messaging and texting mimic this—but it's not the same.

7. When you need to send a harsh email, you can soften the blow (or distance yourself from it) by calling first with advance warning. ("I just wanted you to know that I'm going to be sending you a formal email letting you know that your bid wasn't successful. I value our relationship and hope that we can speak tomorrow, after you've read it.")

Text and Instant Messages

In this realm, the technology is moving faster than, well, the speed of book publishing. It's possible that by the time you pick up this book, the technologies we discuss in this section will be out-of-date, put out to pasture, or so transformed as to be unrecognizable.

When you *text message,* as in the example on the next page, you're sending a written message over your phone. When you *instant message,* also shown on the next page, you're communicating in real time with a pre-existing online contact or community. Both are forms of electronic mail.

> **From: Stanley**
> Where R U,
> Livingstone?

> **From: Livingstone**
> Heading West, U?

According to the Mobile Data Association, text messaging (or texting) in the U. K. has been adopted with enthusiasm. The number of messages sent has risen over 388 per cent in five years, from a daily forty-two million in December 2001 to two hundred and five million throughout December 2006—an average of eight million texts sent every hour. Americans still text message far less than people in other countries, in some measure because phone service in the United States is relatively cheap.

> **Tim:** How long will David go on talking????
> **Dawn:** Forever
> **Tim:** If he says I'M AN ENTERTAINER one more time im gonna smack him
> **Gareth:** At least he gave us that dance
> **Dawn:** Wish we were setting your stapler in jelly or something

It's instant messaging that has been getting America's vote. According to the most recent Pew Internet and American Life Survey, 53 million Americans were already IMing in 2004. (That's 42 per cent of Internet users.) Twenty-four per cent use it more than email; more than 11 million Americans use it at work. PCMag.com reported that at least a quarter of American companies use instant messaging in some official capacity. (Some companies have now turned to instant messaging for *all* internal communication, partly to get around spam—and, perhaps, regulatory oversight.) As increasing numbers of young people, raised on instant messaging, enter the workforce, IM's popularity as an office tool is certain to explode. And that's a good thing.

Having a written confirmation of an on-the-fly conversation can come in handy. Will and his colleagues were in the middle of a tense negotiation. As Will was rushing off to lunch, one of his colleagues shouted down the hall after him, "What should our next bid be?"

Will answered, "Offer 'em seventy-five." What Will's colleague heard, unfortunately, was "Offer one seventy-five."

So the colleague put in an offer of $175,000. In hindsight, Will would have composed a text message in the elevator to confirm his offer—and averted a $100,000 mistake. (Knowledge doesn't come cheap.)

One special word about IM: Many companies have realized that for collaborative efforts, IM technology can be remarkably effective. It depersonalizes the conversation so that people pay attention to the ideas and not who said them; it preserves a record of the session—and sometimes the key insight is evident only when you look back over the transcript; it allows participants to attach photographs and links and other peripheral information.

This can work in other environments, too. Kit Reed, a professor of English at Wesleyan, conducts a writing workshop that takes place entirely online via instant messaging.

(It's called a multiuser object-oriented domain, or M.O.O.) All students are anonymous to one another. (They have screen names.) This setting gives them the opportunity to critique each other's work in a depersonalized—but monitored—setting. "In an electronic environment where people can't see you and you can't see them, even very shy people will say anything. Anything!" Reed told the Wesleyan *Argus*. "For a lot of people, being faceless, genderless, anonymous, is very liberating, especially when they are talking about each other's work."

Five Reasons to IM and Text Instead of Email

1. Unlike email, they always work in real time. ☺
2. Perf 4 shrt msgs. (In fact, they demand them.)
3. They're campfire products—they make it possible for small, self-selected working teams to talk to each other and brainstorm.
4. They're ideal for mobile, silent, and surreptitious instantaneous communication.
5. While they replicate in text form rapid-fire conversations, they still provide a temporary record of who said what when.

One word of warning: People get lulled into thinking that IM's and text messages are ephemeral. Not quite. *Both can be saved by individuals, and IMs can be saved by company servers.*

Mix and Match: Hybrid Strategies

While we've focused on individual technologies, it's important to remember that they don't exist in isolation. You can deploy several in sequence, using email, say, to make initial contact and then the phone to follow up. Or you can combine two or more simultaneously.

If you're responsible for answering someone's telephone, it's extremely efficient if you can IM your boss while she's on a call to tell her that someone is waiting for her on the other line. This saves you scribbling something on a piece of paper, walking into her office, shoving it under her nose, and trying to interpret whether her frantic hand signals mean (*a*) tell the caller to hold, or (*b*) tell the caller to go away, or (*c*) get out of my office.

Or perhaps you are in the middle of resolving a sensitive or emotional negotiation (it doesn't have to be a business deal) on the telephone or in person. It can often be a good idea to confirm the joint decision on email.

Or say you and your colleagues are on a conference call with an outside party. You can IM each other to formulate a unified strategy, comment on what's being said, share visual information, and divvy up responsibilities—all the while carrying on with the call.

A thought about multitasking: The word generally comes up when cultural commentators try to make a big deal out of our efforts to integrate into our lives various tasks that are new to us. So while IMing, emailing, and talking on our phones all at the same time seems like multitasking to the post-forty generation, to most younger people (the generation that's grown up doing all these things), it's really just, well, living.

Linguist Naomi Baron made this point over lunch with Will—a lunch where he managed to take notes, eat his meal, and soak up the atmosphere at a fashionable Washington, D.C., restaurant, even as music was playing in the background. Baron used the analogy of a car. "We simultaneously look forward, check out the rearview and side mirrors, steer, operate the gas and brake, and glance at the speedometer, and yet we don't call this multitasking. We call it driving." Her distinction was between pursuing *single* and *multiple* goals.

Maybe the problem is the word. There is a big difference between sending someone a useful link as you talk to that person on the phone and checking your email during a boring meeting. Maybe we need a special word for the former, for those instances when we direct toward one end all the technological tools at our disposal. Combitasking?

But I Never Got That Email . . .

There's also a difference between *combitasking* (see above) and *duplitasking* (or being really annoying). Most people find it aggravating to get a phone call minutes after receiving an email asking, "Did you get my email?" If it was *that* important, it should have just been a call. Still, it's understandable that people are concerned about whether their emails have arrived.

Here's the good news. Rarely does part of an email go missing. Even though emails are transmitted in pieces (packets), you either get the whole thing or you get nothing at all.

Email is reliable because each packet can take one of many routes to its destination, thereby allowing easy rerouting around trouble spots. But the reliability also comes from the design of the Internet's error-handling system. In the old ARPANET, lost packets were the responsibility of the network: nodes that passed messages to their destinations had to keep track of whether each packet reached its destination. The current TCP/IP system uses a different approach: the onus is on the sender and the receiver—not the network nodes—to make sure that no packets are lost. This is accomplished by having the receiver acknowledge to the sender receipt of every packet. If the sender's server stops receiving "acks," as they are called, the server will wait a short time and then send the problem packets again.

Here's the not-so-great news. In 2005, MIT researchers Mike Afergan and Robert Beverly tested the reliability of email delivery and found that entire emails get lost more often than originally thought. *While 90 per cent of messages reached their destination within five minutes, a few got stuck for nearly a month.* (The researchers also cited evidence that time stamps listed in the header are often wrong because the servers' clocks are incorrectly set.) Moreover, the study found that Fortune 500 company servers bounced back messages sent to a fictitious address within their domains just 28 per cent of the time. This may not be an accident. Spammers can use bounced messages to learn about a company's email system.

In Person

Don't forget to show up sometimes.

Technology was meant to facilitate personal communication—not to do away with it. At the risk of being simplistic: anything done in person is personal. There is enormous pleasure and productivity when we interact with one another. Conventions, meetings, business trips, sales calls, simply walking around the office—all of these activities will always serve a purpose. You only have one self, twenty-four hours in a day, and the ability to be in one place at one time. The very fact of your being somewhere is the ultimate compliment and the ultimate example of your dedication to the work at hand.

Additionally, there's a host of visual and unspoken cues that register consciously and unconsciously when you talk to someone in person. Yes, the phone is far subtler than email, but it's a blunt instrument compared to face-to-face interaction. Which is why there are some things that are far better done in person than any other way; a job interview, a performance review, a firing, and a marriage proposal are just a few obvious ones.

Keep in mind, too, that email was not made for basic decision-making that involves a lot of equal voices. For example, if four people are trying to decide among four different restaurants for dinner, and each has opinions that could influence the others, and the outcome might be dependent on who speaks in what order, then there are 256 possible paths to a decision. If ten people are involved in the same conversation, there are over a million. Here's where a meeting or a conference call can save everyone a lot of trouble.

Even though it can be tempting to hide behind email, the phone, or whatever technology you have at hand, remember to follow the golden rule. Never do anything electronically that you would want others to do to you in person.

Silence

With all these communication tools, it's easy to forget that there are moments when we don't need to send a reply.

Obviously, you should never respond to spam. You also shouldn't feel obliged to respond to "personal spam" (jokes, funny stories, political solicitations sent by a friend or an acquaintance to a large list of people). Profanity, threats, and insults are often best ignored. If a stranger repeatedly emails a question you've already answered or continues to lobby you for a favor you've already told him you can't or don't want to do, it's fine to stop responding.

When a conversation is clearly over, you also don't need to reply. Sometimes it's hard to tell, and there are worse crimes than sending one email too many. But when the exchange has devolved into one-word messages—"Great," "Done"—it's a pretty good sign that further emailing on the topic is unwarranted. You can also take people at their word when they write "No reply necessary" on an email.

And just because everyone else is emailing doesn't mean that you have to email, too. If you're on a group email, you may want to think about whether you're helping or just making your presence known when you add your "Great" to the chorus, or send off that tiny refinement to a plan that didn't really need any refining.

Finally, there are times—particularly in highly contentious situations—when nothing needs to be said. Taking the high road can mean taking no road at all. It's particularly tempting on email always to have the last word, but if somebody has to stop the conversation why can't it be you?

Big Moments in Email History

1976: Queen Elizabeth II becomes the first head of state to send an electronic message.

1978: First spam email. (Sent to every ARPANET address on the West Coast by a marketing representative for a computer company.)

1979: The U.S. Postal Service buys a computer to handle email (and soon sells it).

1983: *War Games* becomes the first major movie to prominently feature email.

1986: John Poindexter and Oliver North dispose of more than five thousand Iran-Contra emails.

1987: First email sent from China to the outside world (Germany).

1992: The World Bank comes online.

1993: The White House sets up its own public email address.

1993: The United Nations comes online.

1994: *Disclosure* becomes the first major movie to prominently feature office email.

1998: *You've Got Mail* becomes the first major movie to prominently feature personal email.

2001: John Paul II becomes the first pope to send an email apology—for injustices committed by clergy in Oceania.

2001: The Taliban bans Internet access.

2006: Britney Spears allegedly dumps her husband via BlackBerry message.

CHAPTER 2

The Anatomy of an Email

We are often so focused on what we want to say in an email that we give too little thought to the mechanics—especially when we are replying to a message rather than initiating one. This is because the To, Cc, and Bcc fields and the Subject line are built into our email programs, so we consign them to a default mode: simply hit one of the Reply buttons, and everything is filled in for you.

This lack of mindfulness also applies to the other basic elements of our emails. Whether or not to forward an attachment or attach flags; what font, point size, and color to use; how to greet someone or close—all these choices tend to get less attention than they deserve. This is a shame, because taking a few seconds to think about how you want to build your email can make all the difference.

Let's go through the building blocks of an email, from the top down.

To:

You've written a brilliant email outlining your suggestions for a project at work. We mean "perfect." Not a flaw. Funny. Direct. Detailed. Precise.

Then you send it to a colleague who thinks, "This is nice. But what does it have to do with me?" Or you forget to include one of the people it *most* concerns, and all your efforts go up in smoke because now that person isn't speaking to you.

We're not talking about *mistakenly directed* emails here. We're talking about your everyday, run-of-the-mill, *poorly directed* ones.

These come in many varieties. Include too many people in your To field, and no one feels obligated to respond. Go over or around someone in your To field, and you can wind up undermining your objective. Bother an important contact with an inappropriate request, and your subsequent emails may not be answered. When you email the sales director for New England with an Atlanta request, you wind up irritating the person you emailed—and, eventually, the person you didn't. The message is either "I don't know what you do" or "I think you're one of those people who will do whatever I ask them, even if it's not your job." Both are bad.

At the risk of stating the obvious, even the most elegantly phrased email won't get you what you want if it doesn't go to the right person: the person who can act on it. Here are some other things to keep in mind.

Too Many

Beware of putting too many people in the To line. If you ask six people to bring a document to a meeting, there's a chance that all six will do it—and there's a chance that no one will, unless you remember in the body of the message to assign specific tasks to each person.

To wit:

To: Joe, Rosa
Subject: The meeting
From: Andy

Can one of you remember to bring the pie chart to the Mr Kipling meeting?

So, who's going to bring it?

To: Joe, Rosa
Subject: The meeting
From: Andy

Joe: Please bring the pie chart to the Mr Kipling meeting.
Rosa: Can you please REMIND Joe to bring the pie chart to the meeting?

Patrick Lencioni, the author of *The Five Dysfunctions of a Team*, told us, "When I send an email to one person, there's a 95 per cent chance I'll get a reply. When I send to ten people, the response rate drops to 5 per cent. When you add people, you drastically decrease the exclusivity and make people feel they don't need to read the email or do what you ask." He calls this the electronic version of the Freeloader Effect.

It's just human nature: an individual is far more likely to do as instructed in an email if he or she is the only person in the To line.

To Is Not Cc

Don't confuse the To field with Cc. For example, if you want to thank one person—but you want other people to know about it—put the other people in the Cc line. If you cram them all in the To field, the person being thanked is likely to feel slighted.

Let's say that you want to acknowledge Tom, one of several people on a committee assigned to draft a document, for having worked late.

Here's an example of what *not* to do:

To: Benjamin Franklin, John Adams, Roger Sherman, Robert Livingston, Thomas Jefferson
From: Second Continental Congress

Thank you for staying so late to finish the Declaration.

Here's what you should have done:

To: Thomas Jefferson
Cc: Benjamin Franklin, John Adams, Roger Sherman, Robert Livingston
From: Second Continental Congress

Thank you for staying so late to finish the Declaration.

Private Addresses

Guess which of these addressees stands to profit from knowing the email addresses of the others?

To: Elvis@Graceland.gov; Lord@Lucan.com; Robert@Maxwell.net; JD@Salinger.com; HotTips@nationalenquirer.com

When you write to a lot of people at once, keep in mind that you are sharing private email addresses with the world—addresses that the recipients may not want to share. (The flip side, of course, is that mass emails you receive can be a great way to add to your list of contacts.) Get a tech wizard to teach you how to repress individual names on a group email list—or put everyone in the Bcc field to preserve their anonymity. And be sparing of group emails.

The Best Address

Many of us wear several hats, and the popularity of multiple email addresses reflects this. Before you send, make sure you're directing your email to the best possible address. (How often have we heard something like this: "I can't believe you sent the message to *that* Hotmail account. I hardly ever check it." Or worse: "I can't believe you sent that message to my office. Don't you know they read everything?") This isn't just to ensure that the addressee gets the email (and that the email doesn't get him fired)—it's also to get your message to someone when he's most likely to be thinking about the issues your email raises. There's a balancing act here between finding people where they'll be *checking* and finding them when they'll be in the *right state of mind*.

It's often obvious which email address corresponds to the relevant part of the recipient's life.

Bill@Microsoft.com: Here's a plan to destroy viruses.

Bill@Gatesfoundation.com: Here's a plan to destroy malaria.

Bill@hotmail.com: Wanna come over for beers on Friday?

When it isn't obvious, you can ask—or send to all the addresses you have, bearing in mind these two rules:

You usually can't go wrong by replying to the address from whence the message came—as long as you're sticking to the same type of subject.

Never send anything to a business email address that the recipient would be embarrassed to have the entire company read.

The Order

More people than you think care about hierarchy. Make sure you put the names in your To field in the proper order, generally according to rank.

It should look something like this:

To: Field Marshall, General, Colonel, Captain, Lieutenant, Sergeant, Corporal, Private

But what if you're writing to a lot of privates? You can go by seniority, familiarity, sensitivity (maybe you want to put the person who cares most about this stuff first), or relevance to the task at hand. When in doubt, you can alphabetize—or decide not to sweat it.

The Accidental To

With email, we are all accident-prone. With the slip of a finger, it's easy to send a message that's half-baked—or even raw.

What's more, if you've used email for, say, more than a month or two, chances are that you have been involved in a redirect or a forwarding misadventure. You think you're replying to someone, but really you're forwarding an email; you think you're forwarding an email, but really you're replying to one; you think you're replying to one person, but really you're replying to everyone; you think you're starting a fresh email string, but you aren't, and what lurks below from previous emails may be mortifying.

Autofill poses another danger. If you have two people in your address book whose names start with the same letters, your email program makes it remarkably easy for you to send the message to the wrong person. Say, for instance, you're a comedian and you want to send your latest Top 10 List to LEtterman, but you don't look at the screen when you're typing in the addressee's name and it goes to LEno. So Dave doesn't get the list and Jay thinks you're an idiot.

Mailing lists can magnify the potential for disaster. In the middle of a computer training session in 2006, the admissions director at the University of California at Berkeley's law school sent the following message to as many as 7,000 applicants: "I'm writing to congratulate you again for being admitted." For the 6,500 of those who hadn't been admitted, this came as a surprise. As did the subsequent retraction that came via email twenty minutes later.

"I was fooling around with the program," the admissions director told the *San Francisco Chronicle*. "I hit the 'send' button and immediately all the blood drained from my head."

At least the admissions officer realized instantly that he had screwed up and had a chance to correct his error. That's not always the case. For example, every once in a while David gets an email from a certain public relations person. Two years ago, this individual accidentally forwarded David a copy of his correspondence with a client who had written an Op-Ed article that had been rejected by David. (Politely rejected, we should add.) The note discussed David's editorial judgment and character with a salty forthrightness that would have both enlivened the original Op-Ed piece and made it unpublishable in a family newspaper.

While David looks with care at every Op-Ed piece (and has, in fact, accepted other articles that have since come to him via this public relations person), it would be dishonest to say that a flash of annoyance doesn't cross his mind whenever this particular name pops up in his inbox. If David were in another field of work, this person's emails might go unread.

Cc:

If you just want to make sure people are kept in the loop, then they don't belong in the To field at all; they belong in a . . . Cc.

What a Cc says is simply this: I want you to know what's going on, even though you probably don't have to do anything about it. Because its purpose is so murky, a Cc is a political and hierarchical minefield.

A Correct Cc

To: Little Brother
Cc: Big Sister
From: Dad

Please feed the lizard.

Little Brother knows it's his job. Big Sister knows not to do it—and might even remind Little Brother. Had she been in To and not Cc, the lizard might have been fed twice—or not at all.

Picking Sides

When you Cc, think carefully each time about whom you want in and whom you want out, no matter whether you're initiating or replying. Just because someone was in on the email exchange from the start doesn't mean that person should be there forever. But if someone is trying to exclude from a conversation someone else who by rights should be part of it, a Cc can set everyone straight. What do we mean? Here's an example of a supervisor writing to a customer (Adrian) who had tried to circumvent a service representative (Leontine):

To: Adrian
Cc: Leontine
Re: The marketing campaign

I'm sorry you aren't satisfied with Leontine's response. But I'm afraid it does represent the company's position. I hope you will appreciate that it's best if you keep corresponding directly with her.
Sincerely,
The Supervisor

Leontine's supervisor could have done this without a Cc, but including Leontine told both the client and Leontine that she had her superior's full support. (In some delicate cases, this would be better handled with a phone call.)

Dropping and Adding as You Go

Unilaterally dropping or adding a Cc in an ongoing email conversation can alter a group dynamic or create suspicion. When in doubt, you can always ask somebody—by phone, in person, or by email—if he minds whether you do or don't Cc a particular person on a piece of correspondence.

If you think that someone should be liberated from an email chain, offer to set that person free:

To: Marcie
From: Lucy
Re: Halloween Special

There may be dozens more emails about the logistics for the upcoming show. Let me know if you still want to be Cc'd on all of them, or if you'd rather we didn't clog your inbox.

Or if you want to add someone:

To: Charlie Brown, Pigpen, Snoopy, Woodstock
Cc: Schroeder
From: Lucy
Re: Halloween Special

Hey guys, we're adding Schroeder to these emails because he's going to be playing piano on the show.

Note: Lucy called Charlie Brown before sending out this second email; she knows that he has low self-esteem, and she didn't want him to take it personally when she unilaterally added Schroeder to the chain.

Escalation

If you Cc someone's boss on a complimentary email, it's a way of enlarging the compliment. If you Cc someone's boss on a complaint, it makes the reprimand much worse. Add the legal or the human resource departments on a Cc, and, if you are the boss, you're sending the message that the recipient's days are numbered; if you're an employee, you've probably just started a war. Ditto if either party Cc's the press, the Better Business Bureau, or a government entity.

COOL

To: Saddam Hussein
From: George W. Bush

Please let in the weapons inspectors.

WARM

To: Saddam Hussein
From: George W. Bush
Cc: U.N. Security Council

Please let in the weapons inspectors.

HOT

To: Saddam Hussein
From: George W. Bush
Cc: United Nations Secretary General, NATO,
European Union, Joint Chiefs of Staff

Please let in the weapons inspectors.

Going Public

Never forget that a Cc has the power to publicly shame some-one, whether that's your intention or not.

Here's a cautionary tale concerning a president of the China division of a many billion-dollar-a-year multinational. One evening in May 2006, the executive found his office locked, which prompted him to send the following email to his secretary:

> You locked me out of my office this evening because you assume I have my office key on my person. With immediate effect, you do not leave the office until you have checked with all the managers you support.

At some point between composition and hitting the Send key he felt compelled to Cc others in the company.

His secretary replied:

> I locked the door because the office has been burgled in the past. Even though I'm your subordinate, please pay attention to politeness when you speak. This is the

most basic human courtesy. You have your own keys.
You forgot to bring them, but you still want to say it's
someone else's fault.

She in return Cc'd the company's entire China staff. The
email exchange quickly found its way into China's press
and became a source of national debate because the boss was
not from China—and his behavior stirred up local fears of
cultural imperialism. It also managed to touch upon peren-
nially sensitive issues, from gender politics to office hierarchy—whose job is it really to lock the doors?

Eventually, the boss felt compelled to resign. But what if
he hadn't Cc'd that first email? What if he'd just sent it to his
secretary and no one else? (Of course, there's the question of
whether he should have sent it at all . . . but that's a different
section of the book.) Then he would not have turned a minor
and private fit of pique into a public reprimand—a loss of
face that drove the secretary to defend herself in an equally
public way.

Note to CEOs

If you are the supreme boss, you can make life easier for
others if you remember to Cc the appropriate people on the
ladder between you and the person you're writing to. This
tactic encourages transparency and cooperation throughout
the ranks.

This can work the other way, too. We had a discussion
about this. David initially thought that if he received a note
from his CEO, he didn't need to share it with his immediate

boss. His reasoning? It would seem untoward, as if he were bragging about a relationship with the big boss.

Will mounted a convincing argument that it's your responsibility to let your immediate boss know if you're corresponding with his or her boss—something best done by phone, in person, or via a separate or forwarded email. (If you were simply to add your direct boss as a Cc on the reply, it might look like a reprimand to the big boss for not having included your direct supervisor.) The key is to keep one's supervisor up-to-date with what's going on. How would you feel if one of your subordinates was carrying on an email exchange with the CEO and you didn't know about it? While nobody wants a braggart around, it's far worse to keep your boss in the dark or give the impression that there are back-channel communications going on. Knowledge is power; whom you share yours with lets them know what you think of them and how important they are.

Why They're There

Make it clear in your emails to people outside your organization why you've chosen your Cc list.

To: Bride and Groom
From: General Manager, Fancy Hotel
Cc: Flora, Nicolas

I'm so pleased you've chosen our hotel for your wedding. I've Cc'd Flora, who handles our flower arrangements, and Nicolas, our executive chef, who makes our cakes.

Both of them will be in touch with you directly.

When you're replying to an email from another company that has unfamiliar Cc's, never Reply All until you know the identity and job title of every person in the Cc field. This is time-consuming to discover—but worth it. Imagine being in a small meeting with a group of people from another company and not knowing who some of them are and what jobs they do? Would you feel comfortable speaking freely? Or would you be so circumspect that nothing meaningful could be discussed? Imagine what might have happened if the general manager at Fancy Hotel had not told the bride and groom who the Cc's were. They might have written something like this and hit Reply All:

To: General Manager, Fancy Hotel
From: Bride and Groom
Cc: Flora, Nicolas

We are so excited about having our wedding at your stunning hotel, but we will bring our own flowers and make our own cake. No offense, but whoever does your flowers is color-blind—and the cake sample we had on our visit tasted like it came out of a box!

Reply or Reply All?

Let your recipients know in your email whether they should reply only to you or "Please Reply All."

The Politics of the Cc

Nobody likes to be left out. But you can't include everyone on everything. This is why Cc's are among the most troublemaking aspects of email. Below is a case study—there's no right answer or wrong answer, just options with different implications that depend on the personal politics.

The Case

You, Sophie, are a chief surfboard designer. You receive an email from a junior colleague, Cy, who copies Ilya, the head of production, and Sam, the head of sales. He does not copy Evie, the head of your graphics department, who should be in charge of the actual drawing.

To: Sophie
Cc: Ilya, Sam
From: Cy
Re: "Cowabunga"

Is this word still cool? Or not? Should it be on the board?

You think Evie should be part of this.

Here are five options:

Option One: The Simple Add (in which you Reply All and add Evie without comment).

> **To:** Cy
> **Cc:** Ilya, Sam, Evie
> **From:** Sophie
> **Re:** "Cowabunga"
>
> Not really. I think it's kind of nerdy. Others?

Option Two: The Add with Comment (in which you Reply All and add Evie, but comment on that).

> **To:** Cy
> **Cc:** Ilya, Sam, Evie
> **From:** Sophie
> **Re:** "Cowabunga"
>
> Not really. I think it's kind of nerdy. Others? I've added Evie to get her take.

Option Three: The Forward (with no heads-up to the original sender).

To: Evie
From: Sophie
Re: "Cowabunga"

Cy sent me the below. What do you think?

Option Four: The Forward with Cc (back to the original sender).

To: Evie
From: Sophie
Cc: Cy
Re: "Cowabunga"

Cy sent me this. What do you think?

Option Five: The Bounceback to Sender (suggesting he resend).

To: Cy
From: Sophie
Re: "Cowabunga"

I think you should include Evie in this discussion.

The Analysis

Option One: The most efficient response when there are no complicating factors (everyone gets along;

maybe Evie was left off by accident; Evie isn't likely to be offended either way).

Option Two: Basically the same as One, except that it alerts the group to Evie's presence. Cy may see it as a rebuke, however, since it reminds everyone that he forgot to include Evie.

Option Three: Could be seen as conspiratorial—Evie might be mad now that her original exclusion hasn't been publicly rectified; Cy might be mad if he later discovers his email was forwarded.

Option Four: Less conspiratorial than Option Three, and Cy could see this as keeping him in the loop. But he still might feel reprimanded for neglecting to include Evie.

Option Five: By far the *safest* course, as it gives Cy an opportunity to say, "Oops, I forgot," or to explain what may be a good reason for not including Evie. But also the *slowest* course—this is the only option that doesn't succeed in getting the message to Evie immediately so she can give her opinion.

If time is of the essence, this may be a moment to pick up the phone and get Cy's verbal OK to go with Option One or Two.

Bcc:

The Flattering Bcc

By their very nature, blind carbon copies are sneaky things. They should be handled with extreme care. Bcc's should almost never be used for communication within your organization for the simple reason that you don't want to talk behind the backs of the people with whom you work. On rare occasions, though, Bcc's are a defensible way of signaling your faith in a colleague. If you are writing to your boss and you Bcc someone on your team, it can show that person that you value his confidence.

To: Michael Schumacher
From: Head Mechanic
Bcc: Tyre Changer

Dear Mike: We are going through tyres too fast. You have to take the curves slower. The guys in the pit are going nuts.

Inside v. Outside

Bcc's can be useful when corresponding with parties outside your organization. Let's say, for example, that you need to keep your boss abreast of your negotiations with another company. If you Cc her on all relevant correspondence, your counterpart's boss will probably feel the need to get involved in the deal. Before you know it, your boss will be dealing with the problem she wanted you to handle. A Bcc can help you avoid this problem.

> **To:** Foreign Minister, Russian Federation
> **From:** Foreign Secretary, G.B.
> **Bcc:** The Prime Minister
>
> Sergei,
> Think we can resolve that caviar trade dispute on our own?
> Margaret

Informing Without Escalating

A Bcc to your attorney lets him know what's going on but doesn't bring the situation to a boil the way it would if the other side knew you were considering legal action.

> **To:** Milo@Miloscupcakes.com
> **From:** Miriam@Miriamscupcakes.com
> **Bcc:** Lawyer@Miriamscupcakes.com
>
> Dear Milo,
> Congratulations on opening your very own cupcake shop. We couldn't help but notice that your cupcakes taste a heck of a lot like ours. You didn't happen to take our secret recipe by accident, did you?

If a Bcc seems too slimy, you can always forward your just-sent email directly to the person whom you might have Bcc'd, with an "FYI" or an "I thought you might want to know this" added to the top. This approach also ensures that you won't get entangled in a Reply All disaster. Keep in mind: If someone who has been Bcc'd hits Reply All, both his (potentially snotty) answer and the fact that he was secretly included in the correspondence are revealed to everyone.

The ABC's of Cc's and Bcc's (and Forwarding)

Cc: I want you to know and I want the others to know that I want you to know.

Bcc: I want you to know and I DON'T want the others to know that I want you to know.

Forward: I want you to know and I may want to add something to the original message and I may or may not want the others to know that I want you to know, but if it so happens that I don't want them to know I want you to know I want to take no chances that they might accidentally find out due to a Reply All slip of the finger.

From:

Most of the time, you can let From take care of itself. But every now and then you'll want to give it some thought. Here are two instances:

1. The From line tells your recipient where the message is coming from and where his reply should go. If you have several email addresses and want the reply to go to all of them, put those addresses in the Cc field—and request that the person you're emailing hit Reply All so that you'll receive the reply on all your accounts.

2. Remind yourself to email from, and direct email replies to, an appropriate address—work for work, play for play. And keep in mind that your address can hurt you. Make sure that yours creates the right impression. Prospective employers and college admissions officers, for instance, look at email addresses. Probably best, then, not to send your C.V. from BeerGuzzler@campus.edu if you want to get that job or that acceptance letter. (Unless you're looking for work at Tennents or hope to matriculate at an institute of brewing.) Also, most email programs allow you several aliases, so you don't necessarily have to set up a new account—as long as you can keep your aliases straight. This is especially important to remember if you have email for different aliases or several accounts coming into the same inbox. (You can send messages from one account, but have replies go automatically to another.)

Subject Lines

The Subject line is the most important, most neglected line in your email. How important? Well, here, in the box below, is an assortment of real Subject lines, which we received on an average day not so long ago. We chose not to include anything involving erectile dysfunction or business opportunities from Nigeria.

Obviously, there's an element of slight unfairness here. Emails have a context, and the name in the From field might offer you a clue to what these Subject lines are about. That said, we found the first set pretty damn mystifying.

Twelve Useless Subject Lines That Don't Tell You Anything

What to do?

??????

Re: FYI

Two things

Great news

Urgent

Tomorrow

"   "

Status

How is this?

Quick question

We would like your assistance

Twelve Useful Subject Lines
That Tell You What You're In For

Rescue Event 4/29 in New York

Comments on the Strat Plan

Join us at the Merc

Tom and Andy's itinerary

Flap copy due

Mom's birthday

Expenses approved

Acquisitions meeting agenda

Missing subscription documents

National Geographic is interested

Movie this weekend with Swift?

Next year's school schedule

A Subject line is how you tell yourself what you're saying. If you're having trouble coming up with your Subject line, it's a pretty good indication that something's wrong with your message.

Will, for example, got tangled up while trying to send an email after an important sales meeting. Because he hadn't budgeted enough time for the meeting, it had ended abruptly—so he felt he needed to send an apologetic email. Still, a lot had been accomplished—so he felt he needed to send an email recapping the progress that had been made. And he had told the group that he wanted a follow-up meeting—so he felt the need to send an email suggesting a new date and venue.

But what to put in the Subject line? Apologies for the hasty ending? Action plan? Next meeting?

Or a combination of these? Though Will didn't know for certain that the group had been offended, he didn't want to take any risks. An apology would have to be in the Subject line. But it couldn't be the only item—that would fail to capitalize on the great work that had taken place. Making the next meeting the lead item would send the signal that Will was big on meetings but lax at follow-up—but it was the item that required the most immediate response, so he couldn't take a chance on its getting lost in the body of an email.

When Will realized he was trying to do too much in one email, he decided to send two instead.

The first had a Subject line that read "Apologies and Recap of 7/26 Mtg."

The second, sent immediately after the first, had a Subject line that read "Next Sales Mtg. on 8/5."

Our feeling about Subject lines is this: always use them. Make sure they say something informative. Make sure they don't sound like spam. Make sure they reflect not only the first item in your message ("your lunch order") but its entire content ("your lunch order and your court date"). And make sure you use specific names that are identifiable to the recipient. (Don't say, "Meeting"; say, "Kaleigh's meeting.")

Remember, email is ruthlessly democratic. It's hard to tell what's important and what isn't. Your Subject line is one of the few cues you can offer a correspondent to let him or her know when and how to read your message. If we hadn't titled this section, for instance, how easily would you have found it?

Oh, and asking people not to read the email you just sent them—Subject: Recall Last Message—is an invitation for them to read it and then to disseminate its contents as widely as possible. In fact, a friend deliberately marketed a book by sending out an email blast about it, followed immediately by an email requesting, in its Subject line, that people not read the initial message. It worked like a charm. Book sales surged.

Same Subject, Different Lines

Re: Meeting

or

Re: Dividing Up Europe
Re: Crimea in February?
Re: Yalta Conference
Re: Caviar, Cigars, Martinis

Help for the Handheld

More people than ever before are checking their email on handhelds, which can chop off the ends of Subject lines. That's why shorter is better and the first words are key to telling your recipient what you're after.

Softball Dinner at Pizza Express

The above gets the subject of a message across on a tiny screen. "Softball dinner" may be all that appears, but if you're on the team and awaiting dinner plans, it's all you need to catch your attention. By contrast:

You are invited to an end-of-season softball dinner . . .

This Subject line will likely be reduced to "You are invited," leaving its recipient temporarily mystified.

Stay Current

Subject lines need to be updated over the course of an email correspondence, not only to give people an accurate picture of what to expect but also for important legal reasons that we'll discuss later (see page 200). Before you send a new reply, make sure the Subject line matches your message and tells the recipient if the most recent email differs from all those that came before it. This is particularly important when a thread veers off radically from where it started.

For example:

To: Tom
From: Ann
Re: Time for Your Colonoscopy

Pirates of the Caribbean VIII or Spiderman XIV?

This email might be opened more quickly if it read:

To: Tom
From: Ann
Re: Movie rental for tonight?

Pirates of the Caribbean VIII or Spiderman XIV?

Re to Infinity

Don't fall into the "Re:, Re:, Re:" trap. These were useful in the early days of email when it was harder to re-sort your inbox and you needed a way to figure out how far along in a conversation you were. Now that you can easily sort by sender and date sent, those proliferating Re's just look like a tic.

How CAN You Tell If a Message Comes from a Handheld or a Desktop?

Answer: You usually can't—unless someone adds "Sent from a handheld" at the bottom of the message. There is one exception, though. If the sender is using

Microsoft Outlook and he replies from a handheld, the Subject line will show "Re" with a lowercase *e;* if he replies from a desktop, it will be with an uppercase *E*—"RE."

Avoid Hyperbole

There are few things as deflating as a message that does not live up to its billing. "Great News" should be great.

To: Arvid
From: Lance
Re: Great news

I finally remembered the name of that cereal I loved as a kid.

Versus:

To: Arvid
From: Lance
Re: Great news

Paul Allen wants to buy us out.

Even more deflating is the message that directly contradicts its enthusiastic Subject line. Here's an actual email that came to Will:

To: All Employees
From: H.R.
Re: MEMORIAL DAY WEEKEND HOLIDAY!!!!!!!

The Friday before Memorial Day weekend is a full working day. If you leave early, you need to mark it as a vacation day.

Subject Line as Message

The email Subject line is increasingly, and rightly, being used as if it were a text message. "The meeting is at 6" can be the entire email and fit in the Subject line. If you do this, it's a courtesy to add EOM ("End of message") after your brief burst of information.

To: Pluto
From: The Universe
Re: You aren't a planet anymore. EOM

A perplexing (and related) development are those really short messages that begin on the Subject line and then are continued in the body of the email—even though the sender could have fit the whole thing in the Subject line. Maybe it's a habit that comes from texting and instant messaging, which lend themselves to short bursts. But in email it's annoying—like opening a big box only to find a puny gift.

To: Message Splitters
From: Perplexed Readers
Re: Why on earth do . . .

. . . you do this?

A Good Subject Line Can Make All the Difference

A colleague of Will's wanted to get in touch with Craig of Craigslist. For those of you who aren't currently seeking an apartment, a new sofa, or advice on dog training or romance, Craigslist is a largely free online classified advertising service. Lots of people send Craig emails.

So Will's colleague did a Web search and found that Craig had recently given an interview in which he had said, "Storytelling is important." She made sure to put a reference to "storytelling" in the Subject field of her email to him ("Re: Yes, storytelling is very important"). Craig replied within minutes. While Craig does have a reputation for responding to thousands of emails, it does seem likely that the note from Will's colleague got *such* a positive response—they're going to try to have coffee when she's next in San Francisco—because it was neither perfunctory nor dull.

Subject lines done. EOM.

Attachments

The ability to attach documents, spreadsheets, and images in many formats is one of the blessings of email. But people attach too much and too often—from files you don't need to vacation pictures you don't want to look at.

Before you send an attachment, you should ask yourself if it is really necessary to do so. Could you just as easily put the material you want to send in the body of the email? Or could you put the information on a shared drive or Web page and give your recipient directions to it or a link that he or she can click on in the body of the email?

> **To:** Reader
> **From:** Will and David
> **Re:** Attachments
>
> We've provided something fun for you to see at
> www.ThinkBeforeYouSend.com/attachments

Here's the case against attachments. They hog valuable server space. They can be hard to view on handhelds. They bear viruses. And some people set their filters to catch messages bearing attachments. So use only when necessary—and please don't get in the habit of attaching your corporate logo or a graphic representation of your signature to every email you send out.

If you *do* decide to send an attachment, tell your recipients what's in it in the Subject line or the body of your email—that way he can decide whether it's worth opening. To make things even clearer, find useful names for your attachments. (Contrast "Franciscv.doc" with "CV.doc.") And remember: you wouldn't fill someone else's closets with your stuff without asking; don't crowd his computer memory with mysterious gigantic files (anything over one MB), which he may or may not want—and may not even be able to open.

The Eleven Most Common Types of Attachments

The *extension* of a file—the three or four letters after the period in the file name—often refers to the program that creates and uses that type of file. The extension generally describes the way a file's data are coded in the computer's memory. Most formats are understood by a variety of applications; some work only with one company's applications.

- **.xls:** a Microsoft Excel spreadsheet.
- **.ppt:** a Microsoft PowerPoint slide show.
- **.doc:** a Microsoft Word file. As with .xls and .ppt files, .doc files can also be created and opened with free, open-source software like OpenOffice.
- **.exe:** an executable file; that is, a file that will run some program when opened in the Windows operating systems (Mac applications have the extension .app). These files should never be sent without the permission of the recipient, and never opened unless you know who sent them, because they have the power to infiltrate and cause mayhem in your computer and any computer networked with it.
- **.dat:** a file containing only raw data, typically unformatted text that includes carriage returns.
- **.pdf:** Adobe's proprietary file format that generally makes the memory allocation of a

document smaller. Adobe Acrobat generates .pdf files whose printouts look the same regardless of the source of the original document. Microsoft Word will also produce .pdfs (under Print, on Macs). Compression with .pdf is optimal for text documents and generally poor for pictures. Text documents typically consist of large fields of white, which can be abbreviated in the computer's memory. This format is best for portability across different platforms. Open-source programs like Cutepdf can also make .pdf files.

- **.jpeg, .jpg:** an image. The extremely popular .jpeg (Joint Photographic Experts Group) format reduces the file size of images by irretrievably stripping them of some (mostly imperceptible) information. This format is best for compressing high-resolution images. The extent of the compression can be controlled by Photoshop, for example.
- **.gif:** another image format, mainly used for photographs, developed by CompuServe for sending images (and animation) across networks. The .gif format will only support 256 colors, whereas most digital images today have over 16 million colors. This can lead to a loss of information. The .gif is most useful for figures and diagrams with only a few colors: the format is currently losing popularity.

- **.bmp, .png:** two other image formats that are more common today than .gif for digital photographs and the like. The .bmp was developed for Windows but many Mac programs support it as well. The .png format typically achieves .gif-like compression, but it does not have limitations on the number of colors it can represent. Both are useful for medium-grade resolution.
- **.tiff, .tif:** Tagged Image File Format, a format that typically achieves little or no compression, so file sizes tend to be large. Like .pdf, .tiff does not discard information from the file (e.g., detail or color in a picture), whereas .jpeg and .gif do. The .tiff is useful for high-resolution images. Another format—with the extension .eps—is also good for high-resolution images. Adobe Photoshop and Microsoft PowerPoint both allow saving files as .tiff, .gif, .jpeg, .eps, .bmp, .png, .pdf, and other formats.
- **.htm, .html:** HyperText Markup Language. A file in this format is one that is designed to be viewed with a Web browser like Firefox. Most Web pages are in this format, and pages saved to your computer will often be in .html. Html is a tagged language—meaning that it is essentially glorified typesetting—and Web pages increasingly make

use of more highly elaborated languages such as Java. Html became the benchmark format for Web pages because it standardized protocol for hyperlinks and allows great flexibility. Browsers allow easy viewing of the source script of .html Web pages.

And beware: it's possible for people to rename file extensions in order to sneak them past firewalls. What looks like a harmless .pdf may be an evil .exe.

Urgent, Notify Sender, and Follow-up Flag:

You should avoid them all. Your email should speak for itself. Urgency and the desire for a response or a follow-up can easily be conveyed in the Subject line and the text of the message itself.

Most programs allow you to choose these options when you're building your email. The first usually attaches an exclamation point or some other emphatic marker to your message. The second asks that the recipient click on a box to confirm that she or he has received the email. The third not only attaches a flag to the message line in your inbox but also can send the message to the top of the queue, if the recipient is sorting accordingly.

The problem with all these options is that they're presumptuous. As such, they can backfire.

Before you use them, answer the following:

Urgent?

To you or to them? People who routinely add Urgent to their emails are like the boy who cried wolf—if everything is urgent, then nothing is urgent.

Notify Sender?

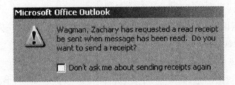

Do you really want to freeze my email and prevent me from doing anything else until I click on the box you attached to your message that lets you know I've received it? (Or, if I check the box that refuses to let you know, leaves you in doubt as to whether or not I've opened it?) To make matters more irritating, if the recipient agrees to the notification, he is, in effect, acknowledging the email, and the clock immediately starts ticking on his response. It's like being served with a subpoena. (Perhaps the only thing more annoying are those Web-based programs—Plaxo comes to mind—that demand that your contacts update your address book for you. It's the equivalent of asking someone to come over and write his name and address in your Rolodex.)

People who attach Notify Sender boxes often find that recipients, out of justifiable annoyance, do read the email but refuse to let the senders know. Keep this in mind: the box requests notification; it's not a requirement.

Add Flags?

Are you certain that your email is more important than everyone else's? If not, save flags for coronations (or another national holiday).

Despite the advice of countless efficiency experts, many people use flags to mark emails they've received and read but want to answer later or reread, turning their inboxes into another to-do list. People who attach flags to emails they *send*, though, may find their flagged email lost in a sea of flags already hoisted by their recipient, whereas an unflagged email would have shown up in the place new email traditionally lands.

Font, Size, and Color

In a recent survey, many employers said they would not interview a candidate if they didn't like the font on his application or cover letter. Even more said they would voice displeasure to a colleague if they objected to that coworker's choice of font.

Now that every computer comes with an enormous list of font choices, it's tempting to try to convey tone, and express individuality, by choosing a more unusual font than Arial (the United Kingdom's favorite) or Times Roman (the U.S. choice). Papyrus, American Typewriter, and **Impact**, to name just a few, all offer an immediate effect, infusing words with added meaning.

Compare the Times Roman:
I have arrived.

The Broadway:
I have arrived.

The Chalkboard:
I have arrived.

And the Blachmoor:
I have arrived.

The first states a fact; the second shouts about it; the third gives a homey effect; and the fourth indicates to the recipient that a necklace of garlic, a silver bullet, and a wooden cross should be kept close at hand.

As tempting as it is to play with the full range of fonts available, it is wise only if you are in a very creative field and writing to people who relish eccentricity. Common sense tells you as much: the medium should never overwhelm the message.

Common sense also tells you that what you write should be readable. Twelve-point type is the norm for business, eight-point is way too small, and sixteen-point and above is inappropriate unless you're writing for cue cards (or for someone who is visually impaired). In addition, what you see on the screen may not be what your sender sees. If you have any concerns, highlight a portion and check it against your font menu before you send it. And hope your recipient has a compatible system.

When it comes to color, stick with black because it's simply the easiest to read. The exception is if you're replying to someone and you need the language you've added to be easily differentiated from theirs. In these instances, go with blue or red. (Some programs do this automatically.)

As for backgrounds or electronic wallpaper—neither is appropriate for a serious message.

Openings

Yo:

Hiya:

Hey, sport:

Fellow residents of Planet Earth:

Sir/Madam:

Dear [Your first name here]:

Dear [Shortened version of your first name here]:

Dear [Your misspelled first name here]:

Dear [Someone else's name here]:

Dear Reader:

The greeting. It's your first, and probably most important, opportunity to show your correspondents what you think your relationship is to them. An inappropriate salutation colors all that follows. You can lose them at "hello."

The Cold Call

People you don't know are always Mr. and Ms. However, the habit of addressing people by their full name—as Mr. Kevin Bacon, for example, instead of simply Mr. Bacon—is one that makes every piece of correspondence that carries it look like a mail-merge document (the bastard child of a form letter and an address book). You would never greet someone in that manner—"Hello, Mr. Kevin Bacon"—so you shouldn't start an email or a letter that way.

There should be no double standards. Men are Mr., and women are Ms. and not Rita or Sweetie. This seems painfully obvious, but we've heard enough stories from women who were addressed informally while their male counterparts were addressed appropriately to think that it bears repeating.

To younger people: if you're writing to someone older

than you are, it's a good idea to address that individual formally from the get-go. To older people: it's not inevitably a sign of disrespect if a younger person sends you an email without a salutation, or with an overly informal one. Keep in mind that many parents and even teachers now encourage kids to address adults by their first names. But you don't have to suffer in silence—if you object, and feel comfortable saying so, let your overly chummy correspondent know.

And if you are going to use mail-merge, get it right. Will recently received an email asking for a donation addressed: Dear <$ Name $>. David has received letters at work addressed to Mr. Ed (as in Op-Ed).

Honorifics

Use titles where appropriate—Dr., Senator, Cardinal, Professor, Commodore, Viceroy, and so on. You are free to ignore all uses of Ph.D. (Word of advice: If you have one, don't put it after your name in a letter. It will generally do you more harm than good.)

Dear

As for the matter of which word should *introduce* the name, "Dear" is always acceptable and always correct. Back when letters were still the main form of communication, there were more variations on this. "My Dear" was used when addressing a close friend or lover. (Some correspondents were strict about never backsliding to "Dear" once a "My Dear" relationship had been established.)

And for centuries "Sir" or "Madam," without anything following, was the proper form of address, particularly when you were writing to someone you did not know. Lord Nelson, in his letters, usually addressed his friends and contacts as "Sir" or as "Dear Sir"—in his entire correspondence, only a few letters are addressed to people by name, and these are clearly to close friends. Addressing a person by his first name is a relatively recent development, and the mark of an increasingly casual culture.

For some reason, people who would never in a letter write "Jim" or "Bob" or "Mr. Smith" with no introductory word beforehand feel no hesitation in doing so in an email. Email is a more urgent form of communication, and we have many more emails to answer every day than letters. But it strikes us as rude to bark out someone's name like that, even in an email, especially if you don't really know your correspondent. Similarly, "Hey," "Hi," and "Yo"—whether solo or preceding a name—should be employed with caution. When Jack Kerouac began a letter with the greeting "Sebastian! You magnificent bastard," he was clearly writing to a friend.

Mr. or Ms.?

Every now and then, you will encounter someone with a gender-neutral name, like Sam or Alex or Chris. In those cases, it's fine to write, "Dear Sam Fox" or "Dear Sam Mendes." In the age of Google, though, there's really no reason you can't do a little bit of research to get the gender right.

Many People

Another frequent email problem is how to address multiple recipients. (When it is one recipient, with many Cc's, then only the recipient needs to be addressed.) Here, the choice of a greeting is particularly important because with it you offer the first clue as to why all these people—some presumably of different rank—have been grouped together to receive something from you.

"Dear Colleagues" is bland and acceptable, as is "Dear Friends" or "Dear Coworkers" or "Dear Customers" or "Dear Shareholders" and the like. "Dear Colleagues Who Volunteered to Help with the Blood Drive" provides information about what is to come. "To Those Who Laughed During the Memorial Service" not only provides information but also sets the tone. There is almost never cause now to write a letter with the classic opening "To Whom It May Concern," which has pretty much gone the way of "Dear Comrades." ("To Whom It May Concern" merely gives the recipient the opportunity to decide that she or he *isn't* much concerned about the subject of your letter, and that it can therefore be deleted at once.)

If there's no succinct way to address the group, there is a one-word salutation that is inoffensive, cordial, and not too casual: "Greetings."

Who Are You?

Email addresses, unlike return addresses on envelopes, often give no clue to the sender's identity. (Sometimes this is intentional; sometimes it isn't.) BERLIN20014@ PROVIDER.ORG won't tell you what to call the person who lives at that electronic address. (Many of us breathed a sigh of relief when CompuServe faded from prominence—those numbered addresses were wildly disorienting.) And just because you get an email from nic@send.edu doesn't mean that you can write, "Dear Nic" if you've never met him—or her. In fact, Nic might not even be the sender's name; it could be the name of the sender's cat or a random group of letters. In these cases, "Greetings," all by itself, has to do. If the recipient is sensitive to this salutation, he or she will sign the return email in a way that lets you know how to address your next one.

How to Say @ in Many Languages

English speakers call "@" the "at" symbol. Some languages have followed suit; others, however, have had different ideas. Here are a few examples, courtesy of the Web site Herodios.com.

Czech (Czech Republic): *Závinač,* which means a herring wrapped around a pickle.

Danish: *Snabel-a,* "elephant's trunk."

Dutch: *Apestaartje,* "little monkey's tail," though sometimes *Apeklootje,* a rude word for another part of the monkey's anatomy.

Hebrew: *Shablul* or *Shablool,* "snail," or *Shtrudl,* "strudel."

Hungarian: *Kukac,* "worm or maggot."

Italian: *Chiocciola,* "snail."
Mandarin Chinese (Taiwan): *Xiao Lao Shu,* "little
mouse," or *Lao Shu Hao,* "mouse sign."
Russian: *Sobachka,* "doggie."
Thai: *Ai tua yiukyiu,* "wiggling worm."

First Names

At some point in a relationship, you will probably make the
jump to first names. An exception is if you have a droll
relationship with someone in the manner of English school-
masters who tend to call each other Mr. and Miss or Mrs.
over the course of a lifetime. A clear indication that it's
OK to move to the first-person familiar is if the person signs
her or his email with a first name only, or puts the first
name at the bottom of the message. Or you can take the first
step.

If you're nervous but also believe that your correspondent
might not be offended by your using his or her given name,
then one tactic is to write, "Dear Pat (if I may)." Of course,
there's something a bit disingenuous about the phrase "if I
may," since you already have, but it nevertheless implies an element of respectful caution. If your correspondent then
writes back using your first name, you will know that the lib-
erty was welcome.

Keep Your Distance

How many times have you received something like this from someone you've never met?

> **To:** Arturo Toscanini
> **From:** Bill Jones
>
> Dear Artie,
> Can I schedule an appointment to tell you about our new batons?
> Bill

If someone in our overly flat (and overly familiar) world has taken liberties with your name—addressed you with an inappropriately familiar salutation in a job application, say—just write back formally, using full names and honorifics. Perhaps then that person will realize he has misjudged his subject.

You might write back thus:

> Dear Mr. Jones,
> Thank you, but I'm not interested.
> Arturo Toscanini

And if someone replies formally to *your* informal overture, take the hint.

As You Were

Once you've made the move to first names, however, it is a mistake to go back to more formal address. It clearly implies a cooling of the relationship. If you do this purposely, it will signal that something so serious has taken place that you no longer consider yourself even remotely friendly with your correspondent.

Going Without

There are many times when it makes sense to send a salutation-free email. A note that was sent without a salutation is always entitled to a salutation-free answer. If a sender doesn't greet you in an email asking for the location of the meeting, it's OK simply to respond with the information, especially as the addition of a greeting might imply criticism at her lack of one.

(It's important to keep in mind that every company has its own internal, and informal, rules. In some places, a "Dear" is often part of an internal email; in others, you rarely see it. And many places really do use "Hi," "Hey," and first-name shout-outs "WILL!" "DAVE!" "ZIDANE!")

Emails among colleagues are generally understood to be part of an ongoing conversation and do not require a greeting. This is especially true when the colleagues are peers. It's less true when you're at the middle level and you're writing to someone at the head of the organization, but again, even this differs from corporate culture to corporate culture. (For instance, at George Soros's institute, most everyone—even some senior employees—addresses the boss as "Dear Mr. Soros" in emails; at companies like MTV, and BT, people internally tend to be addressed by first name.)

Obviously, another time to dispense with greetings is when you are responding to a friend who is so close that there is no chance that you will offend him or her. It's also acceptable to omit greetings in an email that is part of a longer chain. If you write, "Dear Mary," and she responds, "Dear Phil," and you then want to respond to her response, you can just launch right into it, so long as the previous content is sent with your new response. Your initial "Dear" carries over to all subsequent emails from you in the chain, and the same applies with her. If you met Mary on the street, you would greet her by saying, "Hello, Mary." She might say, "Hello, Phil." If she kept repeating your name, or you hers, then it would be, at best, peculiar and, at worst, exasperating. And so it is with email chains.

We must confess that, at the end of the day, when we're trying to respond to everyone who's written to us, we've been guilty of writing back without a salutation to people who probably deserve one. But we've also learned to recognize this omission for what it is—a manifestation of our fatigue and impatience, and a sign that it might be best to log off for the day or get a cup of coffee and start anew.

Sign-offs

Email tends toward informality. It usually lets you know who the sender is—it's right there in the From line. For these reasons, many people, and many corporate cultures, don't use sign-offs, particularly for ongoing or internal communications.

That said, we shouldn't give up on sign-offs just yet. They tell each party something about the nature of the relationship. They also give you an opportunity to let your recipients know how you wish to be addressed. And they can evoke that comforting feeling of writing (and receiving) an actual letter.

There are two parts to the sign-off: the word or words that precede your name, the closing, and the way in which you present your name, the signature.

Closings

"Best," "All best," "Best regards," "Best wishes," "Regards," "Sincerely," "Cordially," "Sincerely yours," "Yours," "Love," "Love and kisses," "xxoo"—all these are traditional complimentary closings used in letters and emails. And all of them, except, of course, for the last three, can be used in formal business writing.

It's a matter of personal style. "Sincerely" is the coldest of the lot, appropriate when you are writing to someone you don't know well. "Best" and "Best wishes" are, at the moment, among the most common in email—safe, all-purpose ways of bringing a note to an end. Many people dispense with closings entirely, leaving only a first name (if that's what they want to be called), or a first and last name, or even just their initials, to close the message.

What's most important is to make sure that you aren't being inappropriately formal or informal. If someone is repeatedly sending you emails ending "Warmly," and you are repeatedly replying with ones signed "Sincerely," then the two of you probably have different ideas about the nature of your relationship. Also remember that, as with first names and cordial greetings, once you escalate a relationship, you send a message if you de-escalate. A correspondent who has been meriting an "All best" may wonder what she did wrong if she suddenly finds herself demoted to a "Sincerely yours."

That leaves the problem of trying to keep track of where you are with each person. There are two simple ways to do this. One is to pick a closing and stick with it once you reach a plateau in your relationship. We both like "As ever," because it means exactly that: whatever you were before, you still are. It's inherently reassuring.

The other strategy is to mirror. But that doesn't help you when you start a fresh exchange, and it can get you in deeper waters than you want. You can quickly find yourself at "Warmly" when you are really only feeling "Sincerely." Complicating this is the sense that when someone is being overly warm to you, it can feel churlish not to return the emotion.

This is particularly thorny at the intersection of gender, friendship, and business. Some people do routinely use "Love" as the closing for all but their most formal correspondence. For others, the word means what it says. It's like that tricky area of social kissing between people of the opposite sex in business situations. Hard to know when it's welcome— or not—and hard to discontinue once you've established the custom. Our advice: start slowly and stick with something safe . . . like "As ever."

Mirror, Mirror

Mirroring or echoing the actions of your correspondent is a great way to overcome email's distancing effects. Whether it's a greeting or a closing, you need to look for ways to build rapport with your correspondent by sounding like him or her.

This is common sense, but it's also embedded in our biology. Scientists have discovered cells in the brain that they've dubbed "mirror neurons." Say a monkey observes you throwing a ball. (It happens to us all the time.) Cells in the monkey's brain will fire in the same way they would if he were throwing the ball himself.

Michael Arbib, a computer scientist at the University of Southern California, has proposed that these same neurons played a role in the development of language, and this theory makes sense. Language is the representation of action—without action. When someone signs, "Warmly," it registers even at a glance, and creates a warm feeling. When you sign, "Warmly," and your correspondent fails to mirror, you may feel a chill.

An experiment conducted by the French psychologist Nicolas Guéguen shows how deeply rooted this impulse is. Guéguen had the idea to test whether a person was more likely to respond to an email sent by another person who shared his or her first name than to an emailer who didn't. He sent fifty university students a lengthy survey. Half the group received the survey from someone they were led to believe shared their first name. (If you were Cary, the email came from Cary; if you were Audrey, the email came from Audrey.) The other half received the survey from someone with a different first name. In all cases, the domain name was the same (their university.com). And the results? Seventy-two per cent of those in the same-name group filled out their surveys as compared to 44 per cent in the different-name group. We tend to respond to those with whom we have something in common.

Remember the benefits of mirroring as they apply to all aspects of your email correspondence: word choice, length, sentence structure, and speed of response. Mirroring is important with regard to content, as well. You don't want to respond to a detailed, meaty email with only frothy pleasantries. Worse, if you reply to the substance of an email but don't mirror the pleasantries, you set a very hostile tone.

To wit:

To: Mike
From: Clarissa

Greetings, Mike! Hope this finds you well. I'm just writing to find out when Noah's television show will

start airing. Things have been wild here; hope you aren't too crazed at work.
All best, Clarissa

To: Clarissa
From: Mike

Dear Clarissa,
July 7.
Sincerely, Michael

Mirroring has a cousin: consistency. Mike's email would seem all the colder if he had an uninterrupted history of long and cordial emails to Clarissa. (And there was that time at the Christmas party . . .)

Oscar Wilde exchanged a lifetime's worth of affectionate and entertaining letters with his dear friend Robert Ross. So when Wilde wrote to Ross, "The entirely business-like tone of your letter just received makes me nervous that you are a prey of terrible emotions, and that it is merely a form of the calm that hides a storm," Wilde wasn't being paranoid. Ross was, almost certainly, upset with Wilde. And he conveyed this not with anger but with a lack of his customary warmth.

If you are given to garrulous and friendly correspondence, you will make your recipients anxious if your messages suddenly shorten and take on a more formal cast.

Signing

You should keep two things in mind if you choose to type your name at the bottom of your emails.

First, as with greetings and closings, how you present your name tells the recipients how you see yourself in relation to them. Henry Ford is different from Henry or Hank.

Second, your signature tells people how you like to be addressed. It's a good way for an Elizabeth, say, to let others know whether she likes to be Liz or Liza or Beth—or Elizabeth. That's why initials can be maddening to a confused recipient.

Signature Block

If you want people to find you easily, a plain-text signature block, without the useless image of your actual signature, but with your full name, title, and contact information, is helpful, especially if the person to whom you're responding has provided you with this information. At some companies this is mandatory; at others it's discouraged, particularly among customer service reps. (In many email programs, you can create a signature block by going to "Preferences" and then looking for "Signature.")

As a general rule, if you are writing to someone, and you want something from her, and you want her to get back to you, it's both smart and courteous to include all your contact information at the end of your email text. If you're writing to someone, and you don't want that person to have all your contact information, remember to remove your signature block before you hit Send.

The Elements of a Signature Block

Full name
Title
Organization
Address
Phone number
Fax
Email address
Web page
Logo
Conversation starter*
Free marketing†
Special relevant detail‡

*At one book publisher in England, employees are encouraged to list their favorite book in their signature block. Other people append quotations, song lyrics, their zodiac sign, and their beloved football team ("Go Wolverines!"), in addition to the other information or instead of it.

†Some companies now use this space to plug—and even show pictures of—their products. ("Look for our newest yogurt flavor this summer!")

‡For instance, people who travel a lot can cut down on confusion by telling their recipients exactly where they are. Tony Wheeler, the founder of the *Lonely Planet* guidebooks, does this. Alerting people that he's emailing from an Internet café in Togo lets them know why they shouldn't expect to hear from him in the next five hours—or why he's not going to be able to make it to a dinner party in Buenos Aires.

Disclaimers

The last decade has been characterized by the growth of Starbucks, organic foods—and email disclaimers at the bottom of messages you receive from lawyers, accountants, and other handlers of sensitive information. We think that these disclaimers have gotten out of control and we suggest, particularly to lawyers, that your ability to disclaim *concisely* will reflect well on your abilities. Some companies have tried to use cuteness to make up for the cumbersome nature of their disclaimers: "Now folks, here's the legal stuff." If you take this approach, make sure it reflects your corporate culture. Or better yet, work on trimming down that language.

CHAPTER 3

How to Write (the Perfect) Email

The fact that email is a searchable, storable medium means that you have to compose your message with special care. And the fact that you are writing—constructing sentences, choosing words, making grammatical decisions, adding punctuation—with previously unimaginable swiftness makes the situation all the more vexed, as does the delusion that email, because it's electronic, is somehow more ephemeral than, say, a letter.

Also, because it's *often* acceptable to be lax about the rules of grammar on email, there's the misconception that it's *always* acceptable to be lax about them. That's not the case. We aren't going to offer a guide to style and usage here—lots of books have done that already and done it well. What we are going to do, though, is outline the implications of taking risks with your English in emails and review the stylistic traps that are peculiar to the medium.

Choosing the Right Words

In Japanese, the status of the person you are addressing governs the words you use. A sentence directed toward a peer, for instance, requires different word forms from one directed to someone higher or lower than you on the social ladder. (You use one word form when speaking to your boss, another to a colleague, yet another to a child.) Learning Japanese, then, requires learning multiple ways of saying the same thing. The need to remember which kind of word form to use is one of the elements that makes it hard for native English speakers to master Japanese.

What many people don't consider, however, is that in this respect English is arguably more complicated than Japanese—precisely because English doesn't offer the convenience of different words to signal that you know the nature of your social relationship to the person with whom you are speaking. In lieu of specific words to show deference—or familiarity—English relies heavily on the delicate manipulation of tone.

More than anything else, vocabulary conveys tone and reveals you as boss or subordinate, buyer or seller, seeker or sage. The words you choose can be formal, casual, or somewhere in between; they can be literal or figurative; they can be precise or vague; understated, correct, or exaggerated; simple or complex; common or rare; prosaic or poetic; contracted or not.

Certainly, some words are inherently safer than others, but if you never venture beyond them you become yet another unmemorable correspondent, ceding the chance to make an impression in your email. Think of your own inbox. When wading through an ocean of emails, don't you yearn for one to jump out? After a hundred people email you that they "look forward to meeting you" so that they can share their "qualifications" or "describe the benefits of their product" or present you with a "business opportunity," you crave something by someone who took the time to choose words with personality, rather than simply cribbing phrases from the modern business lexicon. The trick is to be vivid and specific—even, perhaps, revealing—without forgetting your original relationship with the person to whom you're writing.

On the most elemental level, the deal is this. Before you set finger to keyboard, ask yourself one question (and don't write until you get the answer): *What is my relationship to the person I'm writing to?* Then, make sure your word choice is appropriate.

Ming Lee, age twelve, writes as follows about emailing her friends, whose names have been changed:

> Most emails are pretty short, but they can be fairly long. I've really been only emailing two friends, and they both have a style. Cassie writes short emails and they are pretty rare and are about things like Mangas and trips. Annie's emails, on the other hand, are pretty long and very regular, and we used to have six very long emailings going at once. Those were about six different topics, though boys strayed into all of them at one time or another. Boys, books, boys, trips, boys, sports, boys, family issues, and did I mention boys are

a big topic? And you always end the email with your name.

Oh, and it's almost like an unwritten code that you have to pretty much agree with everything and be totally supportive of what the other person says. It's polite, and if you don't the person will get seriously angry and maybe stop emailing.

Here is an email exchange between Ming and Cassie, followed by Ming's annotations, to show how word choice and style and topic are inextricably linked:

Hi Ming!
My mom is making me do exercises like knee bends and other crap and diet because she says I'm fat. It sucks!!! :(:(:(:(!! But I do like to play basketball, even though I'm short. And i'm pretty good! OMG! I was playing yesterday, when this really CUTE boy rode up on his bike. I missed my shot, but he said it was close and I was really good. And then he smiled this super cute smile and rode off. But he's the first really cute boy i've seen in a while. Where did they go! :(
—Cassie

Hey Cassie,
That was MEAN of your mom to say that you're fat! You are SO not fat!* And stuff like crunches and crap! I'd totally DIE! I HATE exercising, it sucks.† But OMG! You saw a really cute boy!! That rocks!! The only REALLY cute boy I've seen in ages is James, but he is so cute I

don't care. Hee hee!! Maybe you'll get to see him
again, and u can ask him out r somethin. And don't
worry :) u'll see some cuties soon, i bet. oh g2g!
L8ter ;)
Ming

   *You are always nice and totally disagree with the parent.—
Ming
    †Profanity comes up quite a bit.—Ming

Ming again, on emailing her parents:

When teens (me and my friends) write to each other,
it's very different from when we write to adults.
And there's a big difference between kids, teens, and
adults in writing style and topics.

Hi Daddy!
How are you? I'm doing well, but I miss you a lot! The
weather here is all rainy and cold and it's very boring.
It's probably nice and sunny in LA. Grrr, I'm jealous.
I'm thinking of writing another "My Place" story. You
know, the kind that's all descriptive. Do you have
any ideas about what I can write about? I miss you a
lot!! I love you!!
Love,
Ming

See? It's very polite and sticks to the easy things like
weather and how you're feeling. Oh, and no really per-

sonal feelings or boy talk. Plus no, I repeat, NO curses.

Sadly, not everyone is as self-aware as Ming Lee. We've received emails from people applying for jobs who have seriously undermined their chances because their language was too slangy ("Bummer"), too familiar ("Dude"), or simply bizarre ("Right-a-roony").

Also, words chosen to impress, if they aren't part of the writer's spoken vocabulary, usually stick out. A friend of Will's wrote on a college application that the school in question appealed to her "because it is nondenominational," a phrase she had noticed in the college brochure. When subsequently asked in her interview why it was important for her to attend a nondenominational school, she was forced to confess that she had no idea what the word meant. She was not admitted.

Mistakes aren't restricted to applicants. David received this email—from an Ivy League law school PR office—on a day we were working on this chapter. The names have been omitted to protect the guilty:

Dear Mr. Shipley,
I submitted the following as an op-ed . . . several
weeks ago. Considering this is a very
contemporaneous issue, I am resubmitting it to you
for consideration at this time.

OK, so don't use words if you don't know what they mean. The more complicated the misused word, the worse the impression it leaves behind. There's always an element of buffoonery when someone uses a big word incorrectly. Certain words are like Venus flytraps for those attempting to sound grand.

Five Words That Almost Everyone Misuses

Disinterested—impartial and objective (not bored or uninterested).

Irregardless—not standard English; use "regardless."

Nonplussed—confused (not nonchalant).

Penultimate—second to last (not last or really great).

Presently—shortly or soon (not at present or now).

An email with this sort of error faces an uphill battle—which is a shame, because almost every computer now comes loaded with a dictionary and a thesaurus, built specially to save your backside.

Remember, too, that vocabulary is situational. At one company, obscure words might make you come across as clever and educated; at another company those same words would peg you as a show-off. If you're the boss, your words will come under particular scrutiny—more erudite language can signal to employees that you value their intelligence, or it can seem patronizing and pedantic. Whenever you email, you need to make a judgment about your relationship to the person with whom you're communicating and the culture of your company. If you're working at yogurt company Stony-field Farm, for instance, you would come off as overly formal if you wrote an email addressed to "the executive leadership team." The senior management there is fond of cow jokes and refers to itself as "the Moovers."

A moment's reflection—always a good thing when it comes to email—can allow you to replace a word with another that signals more directly what you want, intend, or expect. In an interview with *Rolling Stone*, Sean White, the snowboarder, explained his reaction to winning a gold medal at the Olympics. "I wasn't crying, dude. I had some tears come out." The man who wrote the story claimed this was "a distinction so subtle as to be nonexistent." Really? It seems to us that Sean White was making an important distinction: crying is uncool, but everyone has tears come out.

Misspellings

If careful word choice is the ultimate goal, then accidental word choice is the ultimate pitfall. There is a big difference between poor spelling that reads as sloppiness and poor spelling that results in an entirely different word appearing from the one intended. As people have increasingly come to rely on computer spell-check programs, they've also become increasingly susceptible to creating documents where an entirely wrong, albeit correctly spelled, word has found its way into the text. When the word is obviously wrong ("sned," not "send"), then the recipient will probably guess correctly that you simply failed to proof the document. But when a word is more subtly wrong, then at best she may think you didn't know the meaning of the word you used; at worst she will assume the wrong word was the chosen one, and judge you accordingly.

A computer won't flag "affect" when you meant "effect." If you want your battery changed because it can no longer safely hold a charge, the ramifications if you accidentally ask for it to be charged instead of changed could be disastrous. Will once received an unintentionally humorous note about a film called *The Dangerous Lives of Alter Boys,* except that "Alter" was supposed to be "Altar." The sender intended the Subject line to refer to helpful Catholic children and not castrati.

A friend once received an email that said:

am in Pqris trying to flog q book or 3—bugger French
keyboqrds and forgive the ,istqkes: Will e,qil you over
the weekend: Clips qrrived todqy qnd very many
thqnks.

This is actually a charming example of what would otherwise be a disastrous piece of correspondence. It's saved because its meaning is still clear, it was among pals, and the misspellings are both ubiquitous and cheerfully acknowledged. The point is not that you should never misspell a word, but that you should be aware of how it will be received when you do.

Grammar

Grammar is as important in determining tone as word choice is. The very same words, in different combinations, may or may not mean the same thing. But even if they mean the same thing, they may or may not convey the same tone. The examples used here aren't confined to email because good writing is good writing, no matter the medium.

Bad grammar isn't always wrong. "It ain't over till it's over" isn't right, but it's both memorable and effective. But even good grammar has its pitfalls. A simple sentence can be direct and unvarnished and perfectly appropriate. Or it can come across as childish or dictatorial. A complex sentence can sound conversational or elegant; it can also seem blathering or pompous.

Here's how simple grammar can be used to great effect.

On February 15, 1963, President John F. Kennedy wrote the following memo to Robert McNamara, his secretary of defense, after he had learned that the new military attaché to Laos, a former French colony, had only limited knowledge of French. The memo draws its power from a series of spare sentences, one after another, most sharing the same grammatical pattern, all but the last starting with a first-person pronoun.

I do not see how he can be effective in Laos without knowledge of the language. I would think that the Army must have many officers who have language facility. I would like to receive a report on whether attachés are expected to have a language facility in French or Spanish before they are sent to countries where these languages are spoken. I do not think we should expect an attaché to pick up the language upon his arrival there. Would you let me have your thoughts on this.

The president doesn't say he's annoyed, miffed, perplexed, or that he never wants this to happen again. He doesn't need to, because his disapproval is conveyed by the grammar. The structure is austere; the language is plain; the message is clear. The last sentence, "Would you let me have your thoughts on this," translates to "Please make sure this never happens again."

Obviously, this tone is appropriate for a subordinate and not a peer. But even presidents have peers. When Kennedy wrote to Soviet premier Nikita Khrushchev on the subject of space travel, his grammar turned expansive, complex, almost lyrical.

Beyond these specific projects we are prepared now to discuss broader cooperation in the still more challenging projects which must be undertaken in the exploration of outer space. The tasks are so challenging, the costs so great, and the risks to the brave men who engage in space exploration so grave, that we must in all good conscience try every possibility of sharing these tasks and costs and of minimizing the risks.

In both cases, Kennedy knew who he wanted to be in

relation to the person to whom he was writing—peeved boss to McNamara, visionary partner to fellow world leader Khrushchev.

But what if one of your peers gets out of line? Look at this letter from Kennedy to Khrushchev during the Cuban missile crisis, which echoes the note to McNamara in both structure and tone.

> I have taken careful note of your statement that the events in Cuba might affect peace in all parts of the world. I trust that this does not mean that the Soviet government, using the situation in Cuba as a pretext, is planning to inflame other areas of the world. I would like to think that your government has too great a sense of responsibility to embark upon any enterprise so dangerous to general peace. . . . I believe, Mr. Chairman, that you should recognize that free peoples in all parts of the world do not accept the claim of historical inevitability for Communist revolution.

The Kennedy letters illustrate two surefire grammar guidelines, ones we'd all do well to keep in mind every time we dash off an email that's more than a sentence long:

1. Simple, short, repetitive grammar intensifies.
2. Complex, clause-filled, rhythmically varied sentences generally soften the message.

Please, Thank You, and
Other Insulting Terms

Common sense might tell you that adding "please" or "thank you" to an email will always make it more polite. Common sense would be wrong.

"Would you please remember to include me on the email whenever you respond to a customer?" conveys a sense of exasperation. You've been told this before, it says. Why can't you remember this? Is it so hard?

"Please" is a slippery word. Even though we are taught, from a very young age, to use it whenever we want something, it's almost impossible to use in writing without coming across as obnoxious. The best option is simply to omit it. "Remember to include me . . ." works just fine. (Strangely, the abbreviation "pls." doesn't seem to convey this frosty tone, although obviously it can be used only in informal communication.)

"Thank you" is much less tricky if you remember a simple rule. It's appropriate after a favor, snotty when used before. "Thank you for making sure I got the report" works nicely. "Thank you for making sure I get the report" has an edge to it because it's a command crudely cloaked in premature gratitude.

Punctuation

It's OK to be lax so long as you're on email and on familiar terms with the person to whom you're writing. With handhelds and IMing, the rules are even looser.

It's useful to remind ourselves that punctuation originated as a reading tool. It was developed at a time when anyone who could write wrote by hand. Punctuation was a lifeline in a sea of poor handwriting and ink blotches. But email is completely legible. Generally, you can understand what someone is trying to tell you—even if periods and commas are dropped and paragraphs are littered with dashes.

Still, relaxed punctuation can do damage in a way that heedless uppercasing and lowercasing cannot. Punctuation is in some measure governed by your relationship to the person you're writing to. If it's someone senior to you, punctuate correctly. If the email you received was properly punctuated, your correspondent deserves the same. This is something that's easy to forget. The speed, fluidity, and back-and-forth of email make it easier for all sorts of punctuation tics to creep into our writing. Witness, for example, the (confounding) growth in the use of trailing punctuation. "See you next summer . . ." or "We can just discuss this in the meeting . . ." or "I lost my balloon . . ." We realize that email is often an ongoing conversation, but what's so bad about a period?

And note: any kind of relaxed punctuation is not appropriate in letters or memos. Also, keep in mind that even in email, if you drop, for example, an important comma, you can change the meaning of a sentence 180 degrees.

The Dangers of Missing Punctuation

A friend of ours worked in an office where an email flame war erupted over a missing period. The email in question read:

No thanks to you.

It was supposed to say:

No. Thanks to you.

Paragraphs

Keep them short.

Otherwise, people won't be able to read your emails easily on a computer screen.

Make sure you break a paragraph when you shift topics.

The key point or instruction should never be buried in a long paragraph.

Don't fear white space.

Contractions

Our language comes with an option for paring the fat out of a sentence: contractions. But many people who constantly use contractions in speech will avoid them in writing. The colleague who says, "I don't know whether to get a cappuccino or a latte today," will minutes later write an email stating, "I do not know whether we should send the shipment today or tomorrow." The tone of the latter is more formal and can strike the ear as awkward or fussy; in addition, because it places more emphasis on the "not," it sounds more severe. Email—flat, informal, democratic email—should encourage us to use contractions in a way we'd never use them in formal letters.

In email, *not* contracting comes with a risk. As with so much else, it all goes back to childhood. Parents tend to avoid contractions when teaching small children a lesson. "Do NOT put your fingers in the soup bowl, Elliott (or Ben or Natalie or Sophie); I am telling you that for the last time and I am NOT going to tell you again." The word "don't" is a warning; the phrase "do not" is both a warning and a reprimand. The uncontracted form puts the reader in young Elliott's place, and makes him feel as if he's being lectured by an authority figure. This can be useful when the warning you are giving is dire: the directive "Do not let the nuclear reactor overheat" is strengthened by the use of the freestanding "not." But "Do not make extra copies of the report" would probably be better served by a "don't," unless you mean to suggest that there will be dire consequences for doing so.

And this point isn't confined to contractions of the word "not." Many noncontractions manage to make the recipient feel scolded. The person who says, "I am upset," is probably more upset than the one who says, "I'm upset." In most general email correspondence, the contraction should be the default, the uncontracted form used for special emphasis.

Do Not Not Use Contractions

Here's an experiment: Do not use any contractions in your emails for an entire day. Not only will you find the experience maddening but you may also notice a sudden chill in the ether.

Capitals

When words are written in CAPITAL LETTERS, it means that THE WRITER IS SHOUTING AT YOU. Since no one likes to be yelled at, and people generally shout when they feel that they can win only by intimidation and not by reason, it's a good rule never to compose entire emails in capitals, even cheery ones. For one thing, they're just that much harder to read because we aren't used to reading large blocks of capitalized text. And rarely is it a good idea to capitalize pejorative words—IDIOT, for example. These words are that much harsher when capitalized.

(You can, however, shout a word or two in joy or celebration. HOORAY is a word that is appropriately capitalized. It's a loud word that no one minds hearing louder. Ditto for CONGRATULATIONS and BON APPETIT.)

If you really want to aggravate someone, using all caps is an effective way to do it. A study of email users in the United States and Britain found that overuse of capitals was the thing that most irritated email recipients. (Emails that conveyed an overly friendly tone also made the most-annoying list, but only in the United Kingdom.)

Oddly, writing only in lowercase doesn't indicate the opposite of shouting—no one thinks you are whispering when you abstain from using capital letters. They just think you are too lazy to hit the Shift key from time to time. As with typos and abbreviations, people are more forgiving of this when they know you are sending them a message from a mobile device than when you are clearly at a desktop. There is, however, an implied casualness to all-lowercase communication. Generally, it's acceptable from an employer to an employee but not the other way around, among friends or colleagues, and especially in very short replies. But it's industry-specific—at many companies it's more the rule than the exception. When in doubt, though, capitalize normally, especially if someone wrote to you that way.

I Hate Caps Lock

If you've ever touch-typed a long email thinking that you were using uppercase and lowercase, and then looked at the screen and discovered that the entire thing came out as an all-cap screed, then you'll know the treachery of Caps Lock. This easy-to-hit key can also bite you when you're trying to type a case-sensitive password.

But there is hope. You can program your computer to turn Caps Lock off after a set number of seconds, or to beep every time you hit it. You can even disable the key entirely. To find out how to do these things, just search "Caps Lock" on the Internet. You will find lots of energetic, highly detailed advice about neutering what seems to be the most hated key on the keyboard.

Emoticons

Even though we're well out of junior high, we like emoticons and think there are good uses for them. Pictographic smiling faces and those created out of punctuation marks—☺ and :)—bug many people but they make us smile. (So, of course, does sunshine on our shoulders.) Emoticons are an attempt to put a human face on faceless, quick communication. We also love the whole emoticon family, though we must admit that some of the more baroque manifestations can leave us perplexed—by what they are supposed to be and by when we'd use them. For example, ~(_8^(|) is Homer Simpson and :OI is mouth full.

Emoticons are handy for the following:

1. They're great for text and instant messages and rapid-fire emails because they're really just a kind of shorthand.

2. They're helpful if you want to be cute, ironic, or tongue-in-cheek when writing to those with whom you've already established a comfortable electronic correspondence. Certainly, you can use them with others who have used them with you.

However, emoticons should never be deployed when:

1. You're writing any kind of formal email or electronic message.
2. You're trying to compensate for a barb, a risky joke, or a sarcastic comment; the addition of an emoticon doesn't guarantee that there won't be hurt feelings.

Exclamation Points!!!!!!!!!!!!!!!

One punctuation mark has found a new life as the ur-emoticon: the exclamation mark. The traditional rules allow for an exclamation point only after an actual exclamation—"My Goodness!" or "Good Grief!" Few abide by this any more.

Exclamation points can instantly infuse electronic communication with human warmth. "Thanks!!!!" is way friendlier than "Thanks." And "Hooray!!!!!" is more celebratory than "Hooray." Because email is without affect, it has a dulling quality that almost necessitates kicking everything up a notch just to bring it to where it would normally be. If you try saying "Thanks" or "Congratulations" in the flattest voice you can muster, you'll notice it sounds sarcastic. Without an exclamation point, these may read the same way on the screen.

The exclamation point is a lazy but effective way to combat email's essential lack of tone. "I'll see you at the conference" is a simple statement of fact. "I'll see you at the conference!" lets your fellow conferee know that you're excited and pleased about the event, though this sign of enthusiasm may differ from corporate culture to corporate culture. Sure, the better your word choice, the less need you will have for this form of shorthand. But until we find more time in the day—and until email begins to convey affect—we will continue to sprinkle exclamation points liberally throughout our emails.

A cautionary note: Don't use exclamation points to convey a negative emotion; they make it sound as if you're having a tantrum! And, in serious correspondence, don't use more than one at a time, if you use them at all.

Abbreviations

Abbreviations are like emoticons. They have an important function. FWIW (for what it's worth), PCM (please call me),

W8 (wait)—all these facilitate communication, and in some cases they either help to bond people together in a shared language or are simply taken for granted. Whether an abbreviation seems silly or outlandish depends on where you sit. After all, is LOL, which some people sneer at, really inherently more opaque than FYI?

Of course, when the conversation is formal or you're not sure the other person knows the code, spell words out.

An Email to Remember

Like anyone in publishing, Will receives lots of proposals from people who want to write books. One email proposal, which arrived from a complete stranger, stood out. If you read this portion of it, you'll understand why:

Dear Mr. Schwalbe,
    I am trusting. I got the call today. The call every fireman's wife fears may come. The one I've worried about, prayed about, denied would come to me.
    I am patient. There have been holidays spent at the firehouse waiting for Daddy to return from a call while the kids get cranky and the food gets cold.
    I am nervous. I wake at 3:00 a.m. hearing creaks in the house and don't have the comfort of my husband beside me.

I am tired. The house is full of sick kids and no relief is in sight because Daddy is on a 72-hour shift.

I am jealous. I am envious of all the women whose husbands came home at 5:00 p.m. to have dinner and hold them at the end of their day.

I am grateful. I have a husband who will come home at the end of his shift. Except one day he didn't, November 18, 2002. I got the call: "Mrs. Farren, your husband has been critically injured. He's on his way to the trauma center. Can you get there quickly?"

I am doubting. I am questioning if God hears all my prayers. I am doubting that I am the kind of wife and mother He needs me to be.

I am coping. Often I am lonely, I am surprised, I am underpaid. But in a relationship that defines my identity, I am THE FIREMAN'S WIFE.*

Sincerely,

Susan Farren

*This in fact turned out to be the title of the book, which was successfully published, (Will feels compelled to mention that he doesn't and can't look at unsolicited proposals, no matter how well written. This one was a fluke.)

What Every Sentence Needs: The Truth

Even the most well-constructed email will be at a disadvantage if it's missing this: a genuine representation of who you are and what you mean. Given that email is written remotely and can be endlessly revised, there is the temptation to be less than honest, in ways large and small. In the end, this is a losing strategy. The more we try to be who we aren't, the less interesting we are to other people. Deception is also exhausting. Why act when you can be yourself?

This sounds reasonable on the page, but it's harder to stick to in email. Who hasn't been tempted to alter himself for a new audience? The urge to misrepresent oneself—to embroider an accomplishment or inflate a favorable attribute—can be extremely strong, especially when writing to strangers. Resist. By being dishonest about yourself, you're setting yourself up, in the end, to lose track of who you are.

You will also be found out. Truth in writing shines through—as does falsehood and phoniness. If we had to choose one hallmark of the phony email, it would be excess. Too much politeness, too many big words, too much of anything means that someone is trying too hard. (Tellingly, researchers at Cornell University have shown that when people lie while instant messaging, they use more words than they do when telling the truth. It's that tangled web thing.)

Recently, James Dilworth, the CEO of a small company, posted on Craigslist a plea for applicants to present themselves as they really are, not as they think an employer would want them to be. Here's the point he saved for last:

Win me over by being open and honest. I respect failure, and I look for potential. Yet, it seems to be common practice to BS on resumes nowadays. It's ok to be proud of your accomplishments, but a little modesty makes you look human. I'd much rather meet with someone who admits they've failed, than someone who pretends they've always been successful.

> I successfully led a ten-person team to generate sales of $200,000.

Yeah, OK . . . but I'd respect that person even more if they had the balls to write this:

> In my last job, I had ten people working for me. It was stressful, and I didn't have a clue about how to manage at the time. Two of my team resigned in the first month, and I found it difficult to motivate the other eight who were all older than me. We still met our quota, but I was let go. To be fair, I was in over my head at the time. I have since been to two leadership-training seminars, and I can see now where I went wrong.

Which applicant would you rather talk to?

CHAPTER 4

The Six Essential Types
of Email

There aren't *that* many forms of correspondence. After months of grueling and painstaking research, we've found that email—most essential email—breaks down into six categories: Requesting, Responding, Informing, Thanking, Apologizing, and Connecting. Here are some tricks to use with each.

The Ask: A Guide to Requesting

Email makes it easier than ever before to fire off requests. With the click of a mouse, you can ask anybody to do just about anything.

This is not such a good thing.

Our world is filling up with indiscriminate and inappropriate requests. How many times today were you asked to do something you should never have been asked to do? And did you really need everything you asked for?

Requests are among the most dangerous of all emails, which is why we're going to give them extra attention. The request you can write in ten seconds can take the person to whom you send it an entire day to fulfill. Even a question that's easily answered is an interruption and to some degree an imposition. Permanent wounds can be inflicted in both directions—if your request is inappropriate, you may lose an ally; if your request goes unheeded or unfulfilled, the person to whom you have made it will have burned a bridge with you.

There's a saying in newspapers, one that is particularly relevant in this era of dwindling resources: for every assignment you make, for every reporter you send out on a story, there's another assignment you can't make. After all, there are only so many reporters—and only so much room in the paper. This philosophy should also apply to requests. So before you send an email asking for something, make sure it's something you really need—and something that it's appropriate to ask for.

Carol Weston, a children's book author, received this email from a young admirer, whose name has been changed:

Dear Carol Weston,
Hi! I am Amy. I was just wondering if you can answer a few questions for me.
1. I have a book project that I am doing in school. It is the first book of your series: The Diary of Melanie Martin.
2. I left my book in my locker in school and I was wondering if you can help me out. Can you please

send me a brief summary of the book. I would also like
to ask you if you could tell me what a good
introduction, rising action, climax, falling action, and
resolution is. If you could please help me out, it would
be greatly appreciated.
By the way, I love your books!
Love,
Amy

We think that maybe little Amy was asking for a little too
much.

That said, sometimes it can be hard to figure out what's
reasonable and what isn't; what's tonally appropriate and
what's off-key. Why? People overestimate how well they communicate. What we say is not necessarily what others actually
hear.

A study at Stanford in 1990 demonstrated this point by
having people use their fingers to tap out the rhythm of a
popular song. The tappers were asked to guess how good a
listener would be at identifying the tune. They thought the
listeners would get it right 50 per cent of the time. In the end,
just 3 per cent of listeners could accurately identify the song.

We may think we are tapping out Sinatra and the person
listening may be hearing Sonic Youth. And we may think we
are writing an engaging and forceful email to someone in a
position of power, and that person may read it as intrusive
and inappropriate.

But if you're as sure as can be that what you're asking for
is reasonable, and you think your recipient would agree, then
here are some things to keep in mind.

Orientation

Ask yourself who you are in relation to the person you're about to ask something of. Are you asking your boss for a raise? Are you asking a subordinate to remove his long-expired yogurt from the office refrigerator? Are you asking a peer to take over an assignment that you aren't able to finish? Don't forget, you're *asking* for something: get the tone right.

More Than Email

Consider combination strategies. You can introduce yourself with a letter in which you announce that you will follow up by phone, and then, after that call, use email to answer questions raised in the phone conversation. Email is also great for a save-the-date message, but the real invitation may need to come by mail.

From the Top

Try to put something attention-grabbing in your Subject line. Also, make your request early in the email. Don't assume people will read all the way to the end.

Stay Connected

If you have an "in"—a friend in common who "recommended" or "urged" that you be in touch—your mutual pal's name (and you'd better be telling the truth here) should be the very first two words in the Subject line: "David Evan said I should contact you."

Focus

Ask for one thing. Or ask for lots of things that all have to do with that one thing. But don't ask for several different things. For example, you can ask a dozen questions about apples, but don't ask eleven questions about apples and one question about pomegranates. (Or even one question about apples and one question about pomegranates.) Mixed messages are hard to file, hard to forward, and hard to answer.

Be Brief

Really brief.

But Not Too Brief

Be specific. One of the biggest generators of email traffic is the vague or incomplete request. Examine the following:

To: Owen
From: Fiona

I need to find Rosa.

Now examine a different kind of query. It took a few more seconds to write, but it didn't prompt a cascade of follow-up questions: Rosa who? Where does she work? Who has her number? Should it be left on your voicemail?

To: Owen
From: Fiona

I need to call Rosa at Nor'wester Corp. this week. I think Joe has her number. Would you please send it to me by email? Also, the correct spelling of her last name and title would be very useful. Thanks.

Make It Stand Out

Create space. When you're asking an important question in an email, make sure it doesn't get buried in the text. Keep it to one sentence. Set it off in its own paragraph. Make sure there's plenty of room around it. If you're asking several questions, consider using numbers or asterisks to set them apart.

Start Small

When making a large request of someone's time, it can be helpful to propose a much smaller request first. In 1966, psychologists Jonathan Freedman and Scott Fraser of Stanford asked 144 "housewives" if they would let a "survey team" invade their homes for two hours to make a list of the household products they used. One group of women was asked if they'd be willing to agree to the survey team's visit only after they'd already been asked for a less onerous favor—to complete a brief survey about soap use. The other group was asked right off the bat if they'd open their doors to the survey team. Soap survey plus really big request? Fifty-three per cent said, "Sure!" Really big request all by itself? Only 22 per cent said OK.

Nicolas Guéguen, the French researcher mentioned earlier, found that this "foot-in-the-door" technique can also be applied to email. Guéguen emailed people, asking them to complete a lengthy survey about diets. Some people were asked to fill out the survey after they'd been emailed a simple question about computers; others were asked just to fill out the survey. Again, the appetizer question raised compliance. Diet survey preceded by computer question: 76 per cent. Diet survey without computer question: 44 per cent.

Be Up-front

Don't think you're being clever by masking your request. It is dispiriting to discover that what you thought was a genuine and friendly overture was in fact the pretext for a bald request. Better to be honest from the get-go than to surprise someone about your true intentions.

How to Turn People Off in Two Short Emails

David received this email not so long ago, from someone whose name has been changed:

Hi David:
Hope this finds you content. As I recall, we share Oregon in common, along with our respective stints at [incriminating information removed]. I have my own business . . . and all is well.
One client of mine works near your offices . . . so was hoping to catch up over a cup of coffee on

one of my trips to NYC. Let me know if that is pos-
sible.
Best,
Gary

And here's David's reply, sent with enthusiasm (for
he likes Gary):

Dear Gary,
Nice to hear from you.
That'd be great. Let me know when you know
you'll be up here.
As ever,
David

And here's what came in return:

David:
I will definitely give you a call and look forward
to it.
Until then, can you also advise me on the best way
for [Gary's client] to meet informally with [incrimi-
nating detail removed]? I ask because I do work
for [the client] abroad, but not much in the U.S.
[The client] has been in touch with me this morning
because, as you likely know, there has been deep
consternation about [incriminating information
removed]. . . . I just think he wants to establish a

> dialogue and answer any questions head on; put
> some perspective on their issues.
> Many thanks.
> Gary

So *that's* why Gary was in touch. Which is perfectly understandable, but why not just send the request the first time around? "It's been ages ... hope you're well ... I have a question to ask you ..."

Help Out

Let the recipient know that you will accept the burden of following up.

And approach the recipient at a time that is likely to be convenient for her, something that's easy to forget when you're using email. In our 24/7 world, there's a high probability that she will see your email soon after you send it.

Some business books tell you to make contact at odd hours so that you will be certain to get straight to the IMPORTANT PERSON you're after. Don't. You're more likely to annoy that important person who is using a few precious moments of quiet at the beginning or the end of the day to actually get some work done. And even if you don't annoy, you may catch that person on her handheld, meaning your message may be opened and immediately forgotten. When in doubt, email between nine and five, Monday through

Friday. You can do this even if you write your emails at three in the morning, because lots of email programs can be set for timed release. You can choose this option for one email or for all. (In some current programs, it's under either Options or Message–Change–Queuing, but these things are in flux.)

Keep in mind that people tend to read their newest emails first, even if they still have older unopened messages. So if you are sending multiple messages to the same person, remember that your recipient will probably read the last one first. This means the politeness in your initial email might not serve you if the follow-ups are too abrupt.

This Is Annoying How

A: People read top to bottom.

Q: Why?

A: Bottom posting!

Q: What's the most annoying thing on the Net other than spam?

Be Polite

There's more than one way to be polite, as Penelope Brown and Stephen Levinson point out in *Politeness*—and it's useful to know how these different forms play out in email. The first type emphasizes your solidarity with and connection to the person to whom you're writing. (*We* both know . . .) The second type emphasizes your role as a supplicant. (I know how busy you must be, but . . .) Because of email's inherent affectlessness, a little flattery never hurts, and it's sometimes necessary to be extravagantly polite. But extravagance doesn't work in every situation. Exaggerating the magnitude of the request (I have a *huge* favor to ask) is courteous; exaggerating your relationship (Since you and I go way back . . .) is dangerous and counterproductive.

Being Politic—How to Email a Request to an Elected Official

A legislator friend of ours, by the name of Alison Clarkson, gets dozens of emails a week from her constituents—and sometimes thousands from people around the country, sending form emails at the urging of various interest groups. She reads every email but still worries that requests from her constituents might get lost in the flood. Her suggestions for anyone emailing his or her local, state, or national representative?

1. Front-load the email with identifying characteristics. For example, Clarkson looks for emails that refer to her by name or to a real and current local issue.

2. Keep it calm. The form emails she receives usually start with the phrase "I'm outraged," and rarely with the phrase "I'm concerned."

Follow Up Gently

Be persistent, but don't pester. If you haven't received a response to your request, you can resend your original email.
If you do this, acknowledge that this is the second time
around, and apologize. ("I know how busy you are . . .") Do
not just send the old message again—or with blaming language. ("Why haven't you responded to this?")

Tread Lightly

When you're in a position of power, you have to be careful
that you don't accidentally ask for something without realiz-
ing it. Many of us have been in situations where a boss has
mused, "I wonder how many . . ." or "Wouldn't it be nice to
know . . ." only for that musing to become a research project
that consumed an entire department for months on end.
Even when a boss means to ask for something, she or he
needs to keep in mind what's already been asked, or risk having someone prioritize things differently from the way she
or he might have wanted.

A Graceful Out

The person you're writing to is probably someone you'll want
to write to again. You may fail in your immediate approach.
You may not close the deal. But if you give someone a graceful "out," it also means that you still potentially have an "in"
with them. And who knows, backing off could get you what
you want. Researchers have shown that providing an out—

telling people that they don't have to do something—makes them more likely to comply with a request.

What do we mean by graceful outs? Here are two examples.

For invitations:

I completely understand if you're not able to come. The holidays [or whatever] are such a busy time.

For information requests:

If the information isn't immediately at hand, please feel free simply to ignore and delete this message.

And the all-purpose:

No need to respond to this email.

An Effective Request

Just so you don't think that you have to be a Ph.D. to know how to write an email that states its objective perfectly, read the following message, written by a ten-year-old girl named Emily to her mother. The goal? Get my butt home from camp. (Camp lasts eight weeks; Emily wants to return home at the halfway point, after visiting day.) But also: avoid all-out warfare with Mom. Note the way she states exactly what she wants, and ends with two sentences intended to prompt a positive response.

Dear Mom,
Today was the day of our phone call. I did not like the
way it went. I am very mad at you. I want to come
home after visiting day. I know a lot of kids go to four-
week camp, and will be home by the time visiting day
comes. So I will not be bored at home. Even if no one
was back, I would be happy and excited going with you
to your office every day. I am happy as long as I am
with you. I will make a deal with you: If I really, really
still hate camp by visiting day, then I get to go home,
but I have to try to have fun. Does that sound like a fair
deal to you? It does to me.
Emily

The Answer: A Guide to Responding

It's pleasurable to imagine an ideal world in which our lives
would consist of us issuing command after command, without anyone asking us ever to do anything in return.

Pleasurable, but almost impossible.

Email has only speeded up the flow of requests, orders,
pleas, instructions, and complaints that demand our attention. Because it's so easy for people to ask things of us, they
often do so whimsically and frivolously. Simply responding
to their requests can be overwhelming. Our days are filled
with messages that are easy to answer, messages that are
harder (and more time-consuming) to answer, and some that
are unanswerable.

And make no mistake: people expect a response, and they

expect it to come quickly, no matter how difficult their request. A 2006 survey asked office workers if they would consider it rude not to receive a response to an email within three hours. Fifty per cent said they would. What's more, one in twenty expected to hear back within five minutes. This is probably why more and more offices are making *instant* messaging part of their corporate culture.

In David's line of work, it's the yes email responses that are easy, so these get done right away. For him, there is nothing simpler than accepting an Op-Ed piece. If he reads an article he loves, he can send an email back in minutes, replying enthusiastically and scheduling a publication date.

But what if something is more complicated? He finds that the most time-consuming email responses are when someone has submitted a draft and the writing just isn't working. How to explain this and give constructive suggestions to help the writer fix the problems? Composing that sort of email takes concentration and therefore time—and yet a delay has the potential to exacerbate the situation because the poor soul who wrote the piece is sitting at home stewing, wondering what's going on with his or her carefully crafted essay.

Three Absolute Rules of Responding

1. Answer at the top, not at the bottom, of an email. It's annoying to open a message . . . and not find anything there until you scroll down endlessly in the body of the email.

2. If you're interlacing your response between paragraphs of the original email, make sure that the person you're writing to can tell your words from hers. Use chili peppers, colors, fonts, caps, lowercase, whatever—just make sure that your markings don't vanish during transmission. If in doubt, do a test run with the sender.

3. Check to see that your date and time stamps are correct. If your computer's calendar is off by a year, you'll find that your emails wind up in mysterious places in other people's inboxes.

Tell Them Where You Are

One way to address thorny situations is to be, well, honest. Tell the person whose request you're pondering that you're pondering, and that you'll get back to her as soon as you have something constructive to say. If you want to give a date and think you can stick to it, do so.

Be Fast with Bad News

For most people, it's saying no that's really hard. We don't like to say no—and people don't like to hear it. In this regard, email can encourage our worst instincts. It can insulate us from the situation, making it easier to put off delivering bad news. This strategy tends to end in tears. When it comes to rejection, a quick response is almost always appreciated. The sooner you can get it over with, the better both parties feel. Leaving open the door doesn't help, either. Jack Welch, the former head of General Electric, believes that responding to an email request with an absolute "There's just no way I can do that, but good luck" is a greater kindness than answering with a "Maybe" that's never going to happen.

But Not Too Fast

Two words of warning, though:

First, try not to send bad news late on a Friday. Why ruin someone's weekend?

Second, keep in mind that a really speedy "no" can backfire. If you respond too quickly, people may be suspicious of your response. There have been times when David has gotten a submission, read it, and then sent a rejection to the writer in the span of, say, twenty minutes. Sometimes he'll receive an appreciative reply—"Thanks for letting me know so quickly. Because of your speedy response I was able to place my article with another newspaper." But other times he's received an outraged email claiming that the response came *too* quickly, that he couldn't possibly have read, digested, and fully grasped the ramifications of the author's four-part plan for bringing peace to the Middle East in the time allotted.

Stand Back

Another time to avoid the quick response is when you are just one of the people responding, and others among you are either higher in the organization or more vested in the matter at hand. You might want to see what they say before you jump into the ring. If what you are going to say has already been covered, then hold back. There's a saying on Capitol Hill: "Everything has been said, but not everyone has said it yet." A simple "I agree" is all you need. And often not even that.

Sometimes the Most Eloquent Email Is No Email at All

Remember silence? (See page 48.) While you might think that a nonresponse is so rude as never to be warranted, there are times when it's called for. If someone won't stop sending you offensive communications, despite your pleas, you are within your rights to stop responding. If someone makes you so mad that you feel you can't respond without losing your cool, it may be better not to respond at all.

Other Times When You Care Enough to Stop

The opposite of the nonresponse is the overresponse: people who can't stop responding. For some, it's the need to get the last word in. But for others, it's like the music teacher at the end of *The Sound of Music,* the one who keeps bowing after she's won second prize at the Salzburg Music Festival: they simply can't help themselves. So here's the rule: it's fine to continue confirming and responding as long as there's a realistic chance of misunderstanding. You can even go one step past that, signaling the end of the email string with a "Done." Or an "Agreed." Or a "Great." Then you need to stop.

When You're Really Late

Before you beat yourself up for failing to answer all emails promptly, keep the following in mind: while email has speeded up the world, our correspondence patterns remain the same. Physicist Albert-László Barabási came to this conclusion when he compared the time it took Darwin and Einstein to reply to letters with the time it takes email users to reply to their messages. The famous letter writers and the emailers he studied answered an equal percentage of letters or emails quickly, an equal percentage slowly, and an equal percentage not at all. So much for evolution.

We've all been in situations in which, for one reason or another, we haven't gotten around to getting back to someone. We've all felt that those responses take on a special weight: the longer you delay, the harder it is to actually respond because you have to factor in an explanation for why you didn't manage to do so earlier. Sometimes, the weight gets so heavy that a response of any kind seems impossible.

Our philosophy is that it's always better to send a hideously late response —even an inadequate one—rather than none at all, if you have any interest in maintaining a relationship. In this regard, remember that technology is on your side. The person you've neglected to answer has almost certainly been in your shoes at one time or another. Like you, that person probably has an overflowing email inbox, one in which it's easy to misplace or forget emails. Enough people are feeling sufficiently overwhelmed that there exists a wellspring of understanding if you have failed to answer in a timely way. So fess up. Apologize for screwing up. And just send the damn response.

Five Ways to Apologize for an Inexcusably Tardy Email Reply:

1. I have the awful feeling that I've neglected to answer your kind email . . .
2. I woke up in a panic with the realization that I neglected to answer you . . .
3. A thousand apologies for the slowness of my reply . . .
4. I am a horrible person and a terrible friend . . .
5. I have no good excuse for my rudeness in not answering . . .

Making Up

David inadvertently irritated someone at work, someone he likes and admires. So, while he's not entirely sure that he's been forgiven—it's complicated!—he is now superquick to answer every email from this person in what he hopes will be a successful effort at fence-mending. Requests that might normally slip down on the priority list receive a rapid, and extremely cordial, response.

It's always worth replying promptly and with special cheerfulness to people with whom you've had misunderstandings or difficulties in the past. It's a nice way of letting them know that whatever happened is water under the bridge. Similarly, if you sense someone is contacting you to confirm or strengthen your relationship, a jolly email in return lets the recipient know you view the relationship the same way he does.

Relieving Anxiety

It's a good idea to respond quickly when someone is clearly experiencing anxiety. Emails that ask, "Did I make a fool of myself at the office party?" require a fast response—if not always a wholly truthful one.

Condolences

If you are informed by email of a death, it's perfectly acceptable to respond to the sender by email with your initial condolences—particularly if you think you're going to interact with the sender before a letter would reach him. But this shouldn't stop you from sending a proper letter of sympathy afterward. In fact, your email could say something like this: "A letter will follow, but I did want to let you know right away how sorry I was to hear of your loss."

Invitations

Email invitations seem somehow less important than ones we get in the mail. Nevertheless, in business they're becoming the norm and therefore demand a quick answer. Treat them as you would treat an invitation that came by regular mail or by telephone.

Out-of-Office Assistant

If you know that you aren't in a position to respond—and remember, half the world expects you to do so within hours—don't hesitate to activate your "out-of-office assistant." Every email program has a version of this that can be customized so that it sends a bounceback message like this to people who write to you: "I'm in the office but working on a project and may not be able to get back to you before next week." If nothing else, this courtesy tells people not to read anything into the time it takes you to get back to them.

The Last Re-Sort

When you're starting to feel overwhelmed by all the emails you have to answer, try re-sorting your inbox by clicking on different tabs. If your inbox, for instance, is ordered by date (Received), re-sort by clicking on Sender, and you may realize that there are lots of messages from just one person, which might then be best handled in a single email or a phone call. Re-sorting can have an added benefit of helping you see your inbox anew: emails you've been passing over jump out at you when put in a new context. It's also useful to re-sort by clicking on Size, which allows you to focus your attention on the emails with huge attachments that have been hogging your memory.

(Soon your computer may be able to do this itself, custom-sorting your box in increasingly sophisticated ways. Creating more intuitive inbox technology is now the great space race for software companies—along with improving search and amalgamating all forms of communication.)

And what do you do if you're completely overwhelmed by email? Here, according to *Wired* magazine, is the last-ditch strategy used by Lawrence Lessig, the legal scholar who specializes in all issues electronic:

1. Collect the email addresses of everyone you haven't replied to. Paste them into the Bcc field of a new message you'll send to yourself.

2. Write a polite note explaining your predicament. Apologize profusely—Lessig managed five mea culpas in as many paragraphs—and promise to keep up with your email in the future. Try to sound credible.

3. Ask for a resend of anything particularly pressing and offer to give such messages special attention.

Balance

A final thought on responding: the best way to convey a neutral or generally positive tone is to respond in kind to the message you were sent. A long chatty email is a good way to reply to a long chatty email; a fragmentary answer balances a fragmentary question.

When time or other constraints make balance impossible, it's a good idea to acknowledge the brevity of your response in order to keep from offending accidentally. (As noted earlier, almost everyone makes allowance for terse replies when they announce that they come from a handheld.) Phrases like "On the run" or "Racing to a meeting" or "More to follow" indicate to the recipient that you would reply at greater length if you could, but you can't.

It's especially important to be sensitive to this issue if you feel the sender has labored over her or his opening message to you. Sure, you can always respond to a subordinate's proposal with a cursory "OK" or "No," but that doesn't mean that you should. While the sender probably isn't expecting you to match him paragraph for paragraph, he might still appreciate acknowledgment of his effort. In fact, it's precisely when you are in a position of authority that people scrutinize what you write for clues as to how you feel about them.

Note that this depends in some measure on your corporate culture. If the boss is known for frequently responding with, say, single-word answers, then people are unlikely to take offense when one shows up. If, however, she isn't, they might. This can't be emphasized enough: consistency is key.

Balance doesn't simply apply to length. It also applies to everything else that relates to tone. Any time your reply is colder or more formal than the original piece of correspondence, you could be sending—whether you mean to or not—a distancing message.

Think of it this way.

You email a colleague:

It's always so great to see you, and I really enjoyed the talk you gave at the seminar. By the way, who was that poet you quoted?

Your colleague responds:

Frost.

You start to worry. In fact, you'd feel a lot better had the reply been:

Great seeing you, too. It was Robert Frost.

The Facts: A (Short) Guide to Informing

Because asking and responding take up so much of our email attention, we tend to forget one of email's purest uses: simply informing.

When we're informing, we aren't asking for anything. We aren't demanding a response. We're sharing information, and there's no better way to share information quickly and efficiently than via email.

But people reflexively act on emails, so don't expect them to know they're just being informed (and not asked to do something) unless you make this clear. An "FYI" does the trick nicely. Conversely, if you expect action, make that clear, too, even if the only action expected is for the information to be passed along to others.

This short section was for your information only. Please don't reply.

Gratitude: A Guide to Thanking

A thank-you is pretty basic. Someone does something nice for you and you acknowledge it, right? Sort of. Here are a few tips for thanking on email.

Keeping It to Scale

The thank-you should be proportional to the original deed. Email is a terrific way to thank people for small things. It can also be a terrific way to begin to thank someone for really big things. But in these latter instances, email is only the first shot. Let your recipient know that there's more to come. Suzy Welch, the business writer and former editor of the *Harvard Business Review,* told us that she and her husband, Jack, feel that "sometimes it's not enough to thank by email" and that you "have to back up praise with conversation." She says she's "never seen Jack write a celebratory email without following up with a phone call."

Hit Your Target

Make sure you're thanking the right people and only the right people. If you thank someone who didn't do anything, you cheapen the thank-you. If you forget to thank someone who did do something, well, you've blown it. And if you offer an identical thank-you to someone who did a little and to someone who did a lot you are bound to kill morale with a single keystroke.

A friend of ours once worked more than two years on a difficult project. When the whole thing was over, the person to whose benefit everything accrued sent a thank-you email. A dozen people were involved—some had worked night and day for months; others had just provided an hour or two of advice. Nevertheless, this guy put everyone in the To line on one massive group email. The body of the message said, "Dear Everyone. Thanks so much for all your hard work. I can't tell you how much I appreciate it." And that was it. Here was a case in which the emailer actually *had* told each person how much he appreciated her or his individual effort—very little.

Mixed Messages

If you are thanking someone, don't ask for something else. Thanking and asking don't mix.

A Favor Is Still a Favor

Email makes small favors easy. But just because they're easy doesn't mean they don't merit a thank-you. If someone forwards something for you, or makes an introduction, or emails you information you requested, make sure to thank her appropriately, even if you think the good deed only took her a couple of seconds.

Stop the Madness

On the other hand, don't go crazy. You can thank someone

for a thank-you, but it should stop there. Email thank-you chains have the tendency to go on. And on.

> Thanks so much for your help on the project, Chip. Everything turned out great.
>
> Thanks for your nice email, Dale. I'm so glad you're happy with the final result.
>
> Well, it's thanks in large measure to all your hard work, Chip.
>
> The pleasure was mine, Dale.
>
> Still, Chip, much appreciated.
>
> Looking forward to next time, then.
>
> You bet!
>
> Great!
>
> Good!
>
> Indubitably!

Groveling: A Guide to Apologies

Every rule that applies to thank-yous also applies to apologies. But there's one major difference. You may—and we say may—be able to get away with an insincere thank-you. Not so with an apology. People who have been wounded have their BS meters set at a very sensitive level. Insincere apologies, hedged apologies—neither of these will stick. In this realm, there are times when you will want to avoid email altogether. To really apologize to someone requires truthtelling, sincerity, and, whenever possible, face-to-face groveling. Sometimes nothing else will do.

If you do find yourself apologizing for something serious on email (or by letter or phone call), you'll get a lot farther if you use the active voice (*"I made a mistake"* is much more effective than *"Mistakes were made"*) and take responsibility (*"I'm sorry I hurt you"* is far stronger than *"I'm sorry you feel hurt"*). It will also help if you stay away from qualifications. Watch out for the word "but," which often introduces exculpatory content. And it's always good to *propose* a plan of action to try to fix the damage you've done. Finally, keep it short. It's not about you. (*"I feel so badly I haven't been able to sleep; haven't been able to concentrate; haven't been able to take any enjoyment in life . . ."*) It's about them.

Four Thoughts About Apologizing on Email

Saying you're sorry on email is different from saying you're sorry in other mediums. Before you apologize via email consider the following:

1. *Is email really the best way to apologize—or are you just hiding behind a computer screen?* Here's a test: if you're not even sure you did something wrong and think your email apology is likely to merit an instant and sincere "Forget about it," or a

"Don't be silly," or a "No harm, no foul," or a "Didn't even notice," then email is probably fine. If, however, you know the infraction was more serious, you may want to take your apology to another medium. Why? Because it is so easy to email an apology that people don't always take email apologies seriously. (Not receiving a reply to your email apology is generally a good indication that it fell short.)

2. *Email's speed and ease make it a great way to start an apology.* Remorse is a dish best served hot. Just make sure, though, that the person to whom you're apologizing knows that you'll be saying you're sorry in other ways, too.

3. *Put the word "Sorry" or "Apologies" in the Subject line.* Otherwise, the aggrieved party might not even open your email.

4. *This is one time you really don't want to Cc without permission.* The wounded party may want everyone to know you apologized—or he may want to keep it quiet. Sometimes an apology exacerbates an insult when it's made public. Start focused and then ask permission to go wide. "Please forgive my inappropriate comment in the meeting, and do let me know if you'd like me to apologize to everyone who was there." Also, write your apology with the expectation that it will be forwarded without your permission.

The Email Oops

Email, as we have said, makes all of us accident-prone and many of us impetuous. What's more, the sheer volume of it vastly increases our opportunities for making mistakes. Not surprisingly, the email era has made necessary a special type of apology: the kind you have to make when *you* are the bonehead who fired off a ridiculously intemperate email or who accidentally sent an email to the person you were covertly trashing. In situations like these, our first inclination is to apologize via the medium that got us into so much trouble in the first place. Resist this inclination.

The Three Cardinal Rules You Absolutely Have to Follow If You Are Trying to Apologize for a Mistake You Made on Email

1. *Email got you in trouble, but it probably won't get you out of trouble.* Fall on your sword, ideally in person or on the phone, right away. The graver the email sin, the more the email apology trivializes it.

2. *Don't blame email.* Autofill addressed it, but you wrote it.

3. *Pray that the wounded person has made a similar error and is therefore willing to forgive.*

Social Glue: A Guide to Connecting

We don't just walk around barking orders at each other, or answering questions, or apologizing, or even thanking. We say "hello," we ask about one another's health. It's equally important to do this in email. The most effective emails manage to be clear and succinct but also friendly. This is not about yammering away; it's about remembering to be pleasant—particularly if what you're about to say is in any way contentious or discomfiting. In those cases, it's best to write something kind at the beginning *and* at the end of the email.

That said, some emails exist solely to strengthen or confirm relationships. We're talking about those seemingly inessential emails, where the entire content is the "*how you doing,*" the movie recommendation, the jolly message about nothing that comes out of nowhere. These may be the most essential emails of all.

CHAPTER 5

The Emotional Email

Did we say that email makes us impetuous? Did we say that there are times when it encourages us to go off the rails and write bizarre and dangerous things that we wouldn't normally let past our internal sensors? Does email inspire us to commit to writing our wildest emotions, allowing them to escape into the outside world where they can sometimes do real damage? Does email remove the temporal and physical barriers that keep this from happening in other forms? Did we say that?

Yes. We did. And if you can't remember, then you weren't reading very carefully then, were you?

Oh, sorry. Did that come across as hostile?

If you'd heard us read this aloud, you would have understood that we were joking. (Honest.) But there are times when we haven't been.

Strong emotions are beasts that are hard to control when let out on the page or screen—and because of email we seem to be letting them out a lot these days.

What follows is a field guide to helping you spot—and

tame—the three most dangerous beasts on the email veldt: anger, sarcasm, and duplicity.

Anger

Most of us have on occasion written emails (blisteringly long or witheringly short) that we had no intention of sending. The danger in doing this, of course, comes from the possibility that either out of rage or by accident one will hit the Send key instead of the Delete key when finished. The point is that with email there are few opportunities along the way for your superego and better judgment, self-editing, and cooler thinking to kick in. That's why it's a good idea to refrain from writing angry emails as therapy; but if you must, do it in a word-processing document that can be copied or attached to an email, or printed and sent as a letter—if you decide later that you really do want to send it.

Expressing anger tends to upset the social structure. So before you explode, make sure it's worth it. Do you want to initiate unrest? By expressing your wrath, you are telling your subject that he or she must listen to you. You are no longer equals. You are the aggrieved and he is the culprit. You have the knowledge and he needs to be taught. Everything you say from here on comes from a position of moral superiority. There is a time and a place for this, but you must be aware of the effect of this sort of message before you send it. And you also need to be aware that your outburst may well be forwarded to a much larger community—a good reason to make sure that you want to make your anger public.

In the exchange that follows, a lawyer was so infuriated by the tone of a set of emails sent to him by a younger, less senior attorney that he decided to share the transcript with the world. And the email that finally sent him over the edge was only three words long!

From: Dianna Abdala
To: William A. Korman
Sent: Friday, February 03, 2006 9:23 PM
Subject: Thank you

Dear Attorney Korman,
At this time, I am writing to inform you that I will not be accepting your offer. After careful consideration, I have come to the conclusion that the pay you are offering would neither fulfill me nor support the lifestyle I am living in light of the work I would be doing for you. I have decided instead to work for myself, and reap 100% of the benefits that I sow. Thank you for the interviews.
Dianna L. Abdala, Esq.

From: William A. Korman
To: Dianna Abdala
Sent: Monday, February 06, 2006 12:15 PM
Subject: Re: Thank you

Dianna—Given that you had two interviews, were offered and accepted the job (indeed, you had a definite start date), I am surprised that you chose an email and a 9:30 PM voicemail message to convey this information to me. It smacks of immaturity and is quite unprofessional. Indeed, I did rely upon your acceptance by ordering stationery and business cards with your name, reformatting a computer and setting up both internal and external emails for you here at the office. While I do not quarrel with your reasoning, I am extremely disappointed in the way this played out. I sincerely wish you the best of luck in your future endeavors.

Will Korman

From: Dianna Abdala
To: William A. Korman
Sent: Monday, February 06, 2006 4:01 PM
Subject: Re: Thank you

A real lawyer would have put the contract into writing and not exercised any such reliance until he did so. Again, thank you.

From: William A. Korman
To: Dianna Abdala
Sent: Monday, February 06, 2006 4:18 PM
Subject: Re: Thank you

Thank you for the refresher course on contracts. This is not a bar exam question. You need to realize that this is a very small legal community, especially the criminal defense bar. Do you really want to start pissing off more experienced lawyers at this early stage of your career?

From: Dianna Abdala
To: William A. Korman
Sent: Monday, February 06, 2006 4:29 PM
Subject: Re: Thank you

bla bla bla

The Science of Flame Wars?

Why do angry email exchanges so quickly rage out of control? Dan Gilbert, a Harvard psychologist and the author of *Stumbling on Happiness,* wrote the following about festering conflicts around the world. We think it applies:

> In a study conducted by Sukhwinder Shergill and colleagues at University College London, pairs of volunteers were hooked up to a mechanical device that allowed each of them to exert pressure on the other volunteer's fingers.
> The researcher began the game by exerting a fixed amount of pressure on the first volunteer's finger. The first volunteer was then asked to exert precisely the same amount of pressure on the second volunteer's finger. The second volunteer was then asked to exert the same amount of pressure on the first volunteer's finger. And so on. The two volunteers took turns applying equal amounts of pressure to each

other's fingers while the researchers measured the actual amount of pressure they applied.

The results were striking. Although volunteers tried to respond to each other's touches with equal force, they typically responded with about 40 per cent more force than they had just experienced. Each time a volunteer was touched, he touched back harder, which led the other volunteer to touch back even harder. What began as a game of soft touches quickly became a game of moderate pokes and then hard prods, even though both volunteers were doing their level best to respond in kind.

Each volunteer was convinced that he was responding with equal force and that for some reason the other volunteer was escalating. Neither realized that the escalation was the natural byproduct of a neurological quirk that causes the pain we receive to seem more painful than the pain we produce, so we usually give more pain than we have received.

Our advice here isn't complicated. When it comes to angry emails, ask yourself the following before hitting the Send key: Would you deliver the same message, in the same words, if you were within punching distance?

For instance, is it possible that this interaction between

two financial wizards would have taken place if they had been sitting across the table from each other in a diner?

Take a look. It starts innocently enough.

From: Alan Lewis
To: Daniel Loeb
March 22

Daniel, thanks for calling earlier today. Enclosed is my CV for your review. I look forward to following up with you when you have more time.
Best regards, Alan.

From: Daniel Loeb
To: Alan Lewis
March 28

What are your three best current European ideas?

From: Alan Lewis
To: Daniel Loeb
March 28

Daniel, I am sorry but it does not interest me to move forward in this way.
If you wish to have a proper discussion about what you are looking to accomplish in Europe, and see how I might fit in, fine. Lesson One of dealing in Europe: Business is not conducted in the same informal manner as in the U.S.
Best regards, Alan.

Hmmm. A slight jab? Will it elicit a response? Or will the wounded party go back to his pie and coffee?

From: Daniel Loeb
To: Alan Lewis
March 28

One idea would suffice.
We are an aggressive, performance-oriented fund looking for bloodthirsty competitive individuals, who show initiative and drive, to make outstanding investments. . . .
We find most Brits are a bit set in their ways and prefer to knock back a pint at the pub and go shooting on weekends rather than work hard. Lifestyle choices are important, and knowing one's limitations with respect to dealing in a competitive environment is too. That is Lesson One at my shop. It is good that we learned about this incompatibility early in the process, and I wish you all the best in your career in traditional fund management.

From: Alan Lewis
To: Daniel Loeb
March 28

Daniel, I guess your reputation is proved correct. . . . I did not achieve the success I have by knocking back a pint, as you say. I am aggressive, and I do love this business.
I am half-American and half-French, and having spent

more than half my life on this side of the pond I think I know a little something about how one conducts business in the U.K. and Europe.

There are many opportunities in the U.K. and Europe; shareholder regard is only beginning to be accepted and understood. However, if you come here and handle it in the same brash way you have in the U.S., I guarantee you will fail. Things are done differently here. Yes, place in society still matters, where one went to school etc. It will take tact and patience (traits you obviously do not have) to succeed in this arena. Good luck! Alan.

From: Daniel Loeb
To: Alan Lewis
March 28

Well, you will have plenty of time to discuss your "place in society" with the other fellows at the club. I love the idea of a French/English unemployed guy, whose fund just blew up, telling me that I am going to fail.

At [my company], "one's place in society" does not matter at all. We are a bunch of scrappy guys from diverse backgrounds (Jewish, Muslim, Hindu, etc.) who enjoy outwitting pompous asses, like yourself, in financial markets globally.

Your "inexplicable insouciance" and disrespect is fascinating; it must be a French/English aristocratic thing. I will be following your "career" with great interest.

I have copied Patrick so that he can introduce you to
people who might be a better fit. There must be an
insurance company or mutual fund out there for you.
Dan Loeb.

Here's how it ends. Hard to know who will pick up the
check.

From: Alan Lewis
To: Daniel Loeb
March 28

Hubris.

From: Daniel Loeb
To: Alan Lewis
March 28

Laziness.

All this is not to say that there aren't times when you
shouldn't throw caution to the wind. Larry Kramer, the
writer and activist, often sends long, vivid, impassioned
emails—and he Cc's lots and lots of people. His friend the
writer Calvin Trillin, who has received lots and lots of
Kramer's emails, has a name for them: "Vomit-out emails."
This was meant as a compliment; both writers think there's
a place for this kind of correspondence. Indeed, Kramer
warned recipients of a recent email that it was going to fall
into the category established by Trillin. Kramer opened by
acknowledging that he didn't actually expect the thing he was

angry about to get fixed, and he didn't necessarily expect everyone who received the email to read it, but that sending the message made him feel better.

There are instances when you know that your email is going to make someone angry or burn a bridge, and yet, after careful consideration, you decide to send it anyway. Maybe because you feel the situation justifies it, or maybe just because.

Deborah Tannen's List of Six Ways Women and Men Tend to Use Email Differently

Anger is complicated under any circumstance; gender can make it even more so. As the linguist Deborah Tannen told us (and not via email!), men and women tend to have different conversational styles, and since "the combination of speed and anonymity" in email leads to more aggression, there's more opportunity for misunderstanding than with other forms of communication.

1. Flame wars. Citing the research of Susan Herring, Tannen explains that many men use aggressive language because they find it funny. Since women don't use aggression this way, they often interpret such messages at face value and can be put off or even feel literally attacked.

2. Straight to business. More women than men want to feel there's a personal relationship before

diving into the matter at hand: they expect at least a pleasantry or two at the start of the email.

3. Troubles talk. When women complain to a peer in face-to-face conversation, they tend to want empathy, not advice. When men hear complaints, however, they don't particularly want to empathize—they want to fix the problem at hand. This may also be true in email.

4. Jokes. Men are more likely to send them.

5. Teasing. Men often think it's funny; women are more likely to take it personally.

6. Apologies. Men are far more likely than women to think that an email apology is sufficient.

Sarcasm

Sarcasm may be a less direct form of anger, but it's still anger. The Greek root of "sarcasm" means to rip flesh, usually with your teeth. When a wild animal bites your thigh, it is literally being sarcastic. Of all the tonal choices you can make in correspondence, the decision to use sarcasm should be carefully considered, and almost always abandoned.

We're stressing this point because sarcasm is clearly a popular communication tool—particularly on email, where people are less inhibited and are protected from face-to-face encounters. (It's easy to blame the Jeremy Paxman–Ian

Hislop–*Have I Got News For You* cabal, the age of irony, and the blogosphere for the perceived rise in sarcasm, but really, hasn't sarcasm always been around? After all, the ancient Greeks did have a word for it.)

The *first* problem with sarcasm on email isn't the obvious one—it's that a certain amount of the time, the recipient of a sarcastic message misses the edge entirely and takes it at face value. "Thank you so much for including me in the meeting" is a sarcastic message if you feel you were purposely excluded. If the person who receives the message can't remember whether she invited you or not, she may come away thinking that she did and you just didn't care enough to show up. "Great idea," "Nicely done," "Right on time"—all these can be sarcastic. Or not.

Even in conversation, detecting sarcasm isn't always easy. How many times have we stood, slack-jawed, asking ourselves whether the words we'd just heard come out of a colleague's mouth were supposed to be sarcastic? Sarcastic statements draw on social cues that allow the listener to infer a meaning that is often at odds with the content. As such, understanding sarcasm requires an ability to perceive nonverbal emotional signals from others.

And yet people rarely suspect that their own sarcasm might not be understood. In a study conducted by Jason Kruger and colleagues at the University of Illinois, Cornell undergraduates were asked to write about a number of topics familiar to college students (sports, food, etc.), either with or without sarcasm. They were also asked to report how often they thought their statements would be interpreted correctly by their fellow students—would people catch the sarcasm or not? Participants estimated that they would be understood 97 per cent of the time. They were overly optimistic. Messages were read correctly only 84 per cent of the time. In other words, the students overestimated their success by 13 per cent.

Sarcasm Gone Awry

Here's how a straightforward statement can be read as sarcastic:

A friend of ours emailed his office manager to say that his handheld had crashed.

Her reply: "Oh my god, that's AWFUL!"

His response: "Do I detect a hint of sarcasm?"

And her response: "No, that was sincerity! I know how much you rely on it."

And here's how a sarcastic statement can come across as straightforward. This example, based on real experience, has been fictionalized:

A British journalist friend of ours was working via email with a sportswriter on a piece about the 2006 World Cup Finals in Germany. They started discussing the England squad selection for the championship, in which Sven-Goran Eriksson famously chose David Beckham over rising right-sided midfielder Aaron Lennon, and in doing so forced the team to adopt unnatural positions and tactics. The writer emailed that, by his statistical analysis, Lennon was one of the game's most overrated players.

Our friend wrote back: "So does that mean that Beckham was the right choice?"

That was intended as sarcasm. No matter what you thought of Lennon, nobody in their right mind at that time would think Beckham was a better pick for the team. However, the writer replied earnestly: "No, they could have taken Shaun Wright-Phillips."

That stopped the flow of emails, with the writer obviously thinking our friend was a lightweight on the subject.

The *second* problem with sarcasm is the obvious one: that the object of your sarcasm *will* understand the tone, especially if the sarcasm is intended to provoke pain, not a laugh. People hate sarcastic criticisms because they are the most cutting and condescending form of complaint. If you are a boss and you employ it in email, you may not see the reaction you get, but it won't be one that endears you to your staff. What if you consistently take this tone when writing to a superior? Career suicide. And with colleagues, clients, and peers? Lost sales. Alienated friends. If you absolutely must use sarcasm, our advice is to do it in person. That way, at least you'll have a better chance of knowing immediately if you've messed up, and how badly.

Loaded Phrases and Rhetorical Questions

Sarcasm in email finds perhaps its fullest expression in loaded phrases. These put particular emphasis on your power over someone else and should really never be used. Say these out loud. There's no way you can avoid sounding impatient, patronizing, and sarcastic. On the page or on the screen, they're even worse. Even if the people to whom you are directing these phrases happen to be subordinate to you, will this language really do you any good?

> I can't imagine why . . .
>
> You'll have to . . .
>
> Is it too much to ask . . .
>
> Why in the world . . .
>
> It seems odd that . . .
>
> Just curious, but . . .
>
> Please explain to me . . .

And if you think loaded phrases are debilitating, consider the rhetorical question. We're not talking here about the "Shall I compare thee to a summer's day" kind, but the "I'm asking this question because the answer, if there is an answer, will humiliate you" kind. (The Greeks had a name for this, too: *epiplexis*, asking questions solely to injure or debase.)

Here's email epiplexis at its best—or worst:

Not long ago, our friend Ann (her name has been changed) arrived at work, turned on her computer, and was greeted by this email. Some identifying details have been deleted, but everything else about it is real:

ann,
from what planet do you reside? do you intentionally
act ignorant to your own manufacture of reality? how
can you be entitled to anything when you had—have—
NO CONTRACT with me? is your job in jeopardy? is
your firm's financial position at such an all-time low that
there is a need to leech off me yet again? do the words
"bad business practices" even remotely reach some
level of your intelligence, ethics? for a very long time i
have wondered just what it was that upset me
regarding my dealings with your firm. i finally realized it
via your email—presumptuous. do you know what the
word means? . . . please refrain from contacting me
directly.

Oh, and it carried with it a whole host of Cc's—and
maybe a few Bcc's, too, though Ann will probably never
know.

Here's another classically sarcastic email that Will received. Incriminating details have been removed.

Will,
Don't you think this ad is really unfortunate? Would you
honestly put an ad like this in a newspaper? What were
people thinking? I know you're on deadline . . . but
couldn't someone have shown me the ad sooner?

In one sense, this email was very effective—no one could
have any doubt about the writer's feelings. But it was also en-
raging. Before you send a letter containing questions, it's a
good idea to imagine how the recipient might answer them

without either delivering some clearly unwelcome truth ("Actually, I loved this ad. I was fully prepared to put it in a newspaper. And you've been impossible to talk to for weeks") or utterly abasing himself ("Yes, I do now see that it's unfortunate. I couldn't have put an ad like this in the paper; what was I thinking? And I can't imagine why I didn't show you the ad sooner"). Obviously, these aren't really questions one could answer without admitting to egregiously bad taste, incompetence, and disregard for the feelings of the person whose product is being advertised.

It's instructive to see how dramatically the tone changes when one removes the rhetorical questions:

> Will,
> I just don't like this ad. I can't see putting it in the newspaper. I know you are on deadline, but I need to be shown ads earlier.

The writer's distress is still palpable. The difference is that the humiliating overlay created by the questions is gone.

As a general rule, if a question can't be answered without a loss of face, or if you already know the answer and don't like it, or if you don't know the answer but don't care, then it's not a question; it's there purely for tone. The idea here is not that you should never deploy cutting rhetorical questions; it's that you should know these are dirty bombs that can cause significant collateral damage.

If you can't risk irritating someone, you should never deploy rhetorical questions or loaded phrases. And even if you can, you should first ask yourself (or a professional certified to deal with such questions): Why do I need to assert my dominance over this person?

Does Email Make Us Stupider?

In case you were worried, there is no proof that email makes you stupider. Recent news reports, citing "a study," claimed that checking your email lowers your IQ as much as missing a night's sleep or smoking pot. Wrong. The study's sample? Eight people. And it was a study not about email but about interruptions: participants were asked to solve complex problems while being bombarded with emails *and* cell-phone calls. Not surprisingly, the beleaguered participants performed worse than people who had been asked to undertake the same tasks in peace and quiet.

Duplicity

Not every beastly email is a scream from the top of your lungs or a withering aside. Email can also encourage gossip and duplicity.

These aren't sins of disinhibition or crimes of passion. They're sins of commission. They're the things people do when they think they can get away with them. Lamentably, email makes it easy to engage in Machiavellian dirty work. Knowledge becomes power, to be parceled out selectively. You protect your turf by knocking others down. You share pleasure in the misfortune of others.

Contrast the following:

> You and a colleague are in your boss's office. Your colleague says something stupid. You would love to do more than exchange a raised eyebrow with your boss, but you don't dare. By the time the meeting is over—when a private dissection of the stupid comment might be possible—the moment has passed. Soon, the comment is forgotten.

or

> You are in your office when you and a colleague get an email from your boss. Your colleague replies to you both with a stupid comment. You immediately email your boss (and only your boss) to express your exasperation. It's a bonding moment for you and your boss, but at the expense of someone else. (If bosses weren't human, they might discourage this kind of behavior.)

A Few Words on Being Mean

If you're going to be mean, it's best not to do it on email, for practical reasons as well as cosmic ones.

Richard Phillips, a London lawyer specializing in, yes, computer law and electronic commerce, was having lunch when Jenny Amner, a secretary at his firm, accidentally spilled ketchup on his pants.

After the incident, Phillips felt compelled to send the following email to Amner:

> Hi Jenny, I went to a dry cleaners at lunch and they said it would cost £4 to remove the ketchup stains. If you cd let me have the cash today, that wd be much appreciated. Thanks Richard.

When he didn't receive a prompt response, he continued to pursue the case, including having a colleague leave a Post-it note on Amner's desk reminding her of the debt.

Then Amner responded by email, and Cc'd hundreds of people in her firm:

> **Subject:** Re: Ketchup trousers.
>
> With reference to the email below, I must apologize for not getting back to you straight away but due to my mother's sudden illness, death and funeral I have had more pressing issues than your £4.
> I apologize again for accidentally getting a few splashes of ketchup on your trousers. Obviously your financial need as a senior associate is greater than mine as a mere secretary.
> Having already spoken to and shown your email and Anne-Marie's note to various partners, lawyers and trainees in ECC&T and IP/IT, they kindly offered to do a collection to raise the £4.
> I however declined their kind offer but should you feel the urgent need for the £4, it will be on my desk this afternoon. Jenny.

If this hadn't been on email, it wouldn't have found its way into British newspapers—and into this book.

Getting Email Back

OK. You just sent a really mean, stupid email to someone and you'd like to retrieve it before he sees it. Is this possible?

Well, yes and no.

In theory, your systems *could* be configured to allow you to remove your ill-conceived message from the recipient's mail server at any point before she has read it. But the ability to destroy mail that has arrived at its destination would mean that nobody's email would be safe. Essentially, if you can go into your correspondent's mail server and bring your mail back, you can do much worse.

Some email providers have found a way around this problem. AOL, for example, offers Webmail that provides an Unsend feature. AOL users who send email to others within the same system can unsend or modify their sent messages up until the moment the recipient reads them. Messages between users don't leave the company's servers, so AOL was able to develop a proprietary way to recall messages in-house, so to speak.

If you happen to be using Outlook, AND if both you and the person you're writing to use Microsoft

Exchange Server or a shared company server, AND if the message hasn't yet been opened, you just might be able to retract that stupendously awful email if you do the following:

Open the Sent Items folder, and double-click your message to open it. Then go to Actions and click on Recall This Message. You'll be given the choice to delete the message or replace it with a fresh one if it hasn't been read. However, you cannot completely trust Outlook when it tells you, "No recipients have reported reading this message." It may be that the recipients don't use Outlook, or maybe they don't share your server. The program can't tell you. The messages may well have been received and read.

How to Stay Out of Trouble

The rules for handling emotionally volatile material on email are not all that difficult:

If you wouldn't make the comment to the other person's face and stick around for the response, you probably shouldn't put it in an email.

And it's hard to imagine too many situations when you need to recall a nice message.

CHAPTER 6

The Email That Can Land You in Jail

We operate under the illusion that email communication is intimate and ephemeral.

It's not. It's easily made public and it can live forever. The consequences of forgetting this can be devastating—whether you work for a FTSE 100 corporation, a small business, a not-for-profit, or are on your own.

As soon as there was email, people were getting fired for using it incorrectly. Best we can tell, the first highly publicized, self-inflicted email catastrophe took place at the William Morris Agency in Los Angeles in 1992. Six employees were sacked after they accidentally forwarded messages disparaging the character of executives at their firm. This may have been the first incident, but it certainly hasn't been the last.

And it's not just *your* job you can torpedo—what you put in email can help sink a whole company. Think Enron. Think Merck, where the discovery of smoking gun emails in those Vioxx-related lawsuits helped cost the company roughly $30 billion of its market capitalization. In the last decade, the number of corporate lawsuits in which illegal, mishandled, or inappropriate electronic correspondence became a key piece of evidence has grown exponentially. Not surprisingly, the electronic discovery business is booming, jumping from $500 million in 2003 to $2 billion in 2005.

The email below, sent by one employee to another at a company that makes a controversial diet drug, was used in a civil suit for wrongful death caused by side effects of the diet medication.

> Do I have to look forward to spending my waning years writing checks to fat people worried about a silly lung problem?

And this one comes to us from the case files of a company that analyzes emails in corporate lawsuits:

> Did we get this illegal stuff about withholding expenses and retirement money worked out?

We presume that you are not a criminal. Consequently, this chapter will *not* be devoted to emails that are evidence of a crime—insider trading tips, fraudulent schemes, maps showing where the bodies are buried. Instead we will try to point out some less obvious traps. Email has a special ability to make it look as though you're breaking the law even when you're not.

The Email That Appears Criminal but Isn't

A company called Cataphora, which helps lawyers analyze and review emails in cases where millions of emails need to be scrutinized, found this in a legal investigation:

> Can we talk about that thing we talked about the other day when we spoke about that other thing? When I was visiting you. It is quite urgent.

Sounds pretty suspicious, doesn't it? But "that thing" could have been a surprise party for someone's retirement. In court, however, this email is bound to look like evidence of a conspiracy. (This is why email strings are so important: context is king.)

The software that allows lawyers to search for smoking gun emails is sophisticated. Cataphora's, for example, doesn't just look for "hot" words (Al Qaeda, insider trading, a particular product name). It looks for "worried" language: phrases like "can't sleep," "high blood pressure," "confused and bewildered." It also looks for word combinations that appear to be hiding something—see "that other thing" above.

What's more, it looks for abrupt shifts in personal email style: an accountant who never used exclamation marks or all caps starts using them all the time; a banker who never emails at night suddenly is sending messages at three in the morning; a stockbroker who used to forward emails with only a short note now forwards them with detailed instructions. It even looks for "two-faced" behavior, comparing different cover notes on the same email forwarded to different people.

Current software also looks for traffic patterns. Suppose you drop a colleague from your email list. Did you drop him because you didn't want to bother him—or because you didn't want him to have the information he needed to do his job? If it's the former, and somehow he winds up getting fired, and sues, your email behavior and emails could become part of the case. Or imagine how suspicious it would look if you worked at a financial firm and didn't invite your compliance officer to a key meeting. (A way to avoid such mistakes is to have a pre-set address list for each team or working group—that way nobody gets cut out of the loop by mistake.)

Advice: Be consistent in how you write your emails, whom you include, and when you send them.

Stupid (and Real) Email Phrases That Wound Up in Court*

1. DELETE THIS EMAIL!

2. Do NOT tell Joe.

3. Can we get away with it?

4. They'll never find out.

5. I have serious concerns.

6. I don't care what the hell you do.

7. This might not be legal.

*Courtesy of Cataphora.

The Email That Asks Questions That Can Come Back to Haunt You

When is a question not just a question? When it's asked on email.

The following email was a smoking gun in a court case:

I am very uncomfortable with how these transactions were handled. What do you think I should do about it?

Questions like this can have legal ramifications. For example, if you're a scientist at a drug company, musing about whether you should perform a certain test on your company's wonder drug, you are pretty much obligated to go through with that test once you've asked about it on email. If you don't and something subsequently goes wrong with the medication, your email could be all the proof anyone needs of nefarious intent or careless neglect.

We're not saying never to ask a question again. We're simply saying that even an innocent, well-intentioned question on email can become part of the permanent record, and set off a cascade of unintended consequences.

To illustrate this point, a friend of Will's cites what he has come to call the "$5,000 email." Whenever anyone who reports to him asks by email if something needs a "legal review," it means that the company had better get one—whether or not a $5,000 legal reading was strictly necessary.

Advice: There are certain constructions to watch out for if you're writing on a potentially sensitive matter. If you find yourself emailing, "Do you REALLY think it's a good idea to . . . ?" be aware that it's implicit that you think it isn't. Phrasing your concern as a question won't get you off the hook later on.

Privacy at Work

What follows are excerpts from the policy of a major multinational media corporation (its name has been changed to "Big Corporation"):

> We expect you to use reasonable judgment and discretion when using Big Corporation assets (including systems, files, books and records). You should not transact any significant personal business on Big Corporation premises, on Big Corporation time or using Big Corporation equipment or personnel (whether on staff or otherwise). Big Corporation work facilities, property and supplies, including its computer systems and the files maintained and used by such electronic systems (e.g., electronic mail system, voicemail and computer files) regardless of password protection, telephones, photocopying facilities, mailroom, stationery, trademarks and logos, all are Big Corporation property and are provided to you for the performance of your duties for Big Corporation . . .

We expect you to use Big Corporation's electronic systems for proper business purposes. For example, you should never send an email if you would not put the same words in a letter or memo or would not want them to be viewed as part of a lawsuit or investigation and you should never use email (or other electronic communications) to distribute offensive, vulgar, or pornographic material. We understand that some personal use of Big Corporation's electronic systems may be inevitable. We expect you to keep such use to a reasonable minimum. You should bear in mind that even personal data on Big Corporation systems is subject to these policies. Our systems may not be used to send or forward content that violates our anti-discrimination or anti-harassment policies or for any purpose that is misleading, dishonest, or otherwise improper. While it is impossible to specify every potentially improper use of Big Corporation's electronic systems, examples would include sending an email that appears to be from a person other than yourself or which masks the true identity of the sender or accessing electronic files other than your own or those directly related to your work, even if you have password access to additional files.

Email and voicemail are not private communications. While Big Corporation does not intend to routinely monitor the contents of email or voicemail messages, Big Corporation does reserve the right to have authorized persons inspect or review any data stored in its systems (including computer, email and voicemail systems), all mail sent to or from Big Corporation business addresses, and all Big Corporation offices, furniture, fixtures, files, or other property. Accordingly, you should not use the email or voicemail system for any communication you expect to remain private or personal.

Find this unusual? It isn't.

Fact: Most companies are actively monitoring employee emails—even when you are emailing on your personal account. According to the American Management Association and the ePolicy Institute, 36 per cent of employers are using software to track content, keystrokes, and time spent at the keyboard; and 38 per cent have people whose job it is to monitor your email. Overall, more than half of those employers surveyed said they had either fired or disciplined workers who failed to follow email policy.

So what's the bottom line on checking your private email accounts while you are at work? We asked the human resources director of another large multinational and she confirmed that there's no technological way for her firm to check email messages you've *already* sent using a personal Web-based account—

short of getting a subpoena to present to, say, AOL. But if your company suspects you of being up to no good, it can monitor the personal account emails you are *now* sending as you send them (using, for example, keystroke capture). And if the corporate policy states employees aren't allowed any personal use of the computers, the company doesn't need any legal permission at all. Her advice: don't put anything in a personal email sent from a company computer that you wouldn't want the HR department to read.

The Email That's Not So Funny

Did you hear the one about the guy who forwarded the funny email to everyone in his department?

He got fired!

Ha!

People frequently use email to send jokes. This is a dangerous habit. At best, jokes offer fleeting amusement; at worst, they provide powerful evidence of a hostile workplace. (The law quite sensibly holds that no person should have to work in this sort of environment.)

And yet, people persist. According to a survey by the American Management Association and the ePolicy Institute, 60 per cent of email users admit to having sent email with adult content at work; 50 per cent said they have received email, some of it meant as humor, that was racist, sexist, pornographic, or somehow disparaging.

These findings are borne out in other ways. As part of Enron's giant fraud case, a huge number of the firm's emails were made public. This searchable archive provides a window into the electronic life of an American corporation. A company called InBoxer did a study of the Enron archive and discovered that one out of every twenty-five messages in the database—or 20,378 in all—contained "pornographic content, racially or ethnically offensive language, dirty jokes, or questionable images."

There are plenty of moral and ethical reasons not to send (or tolerate) offensive emails in the workplace. And there are financial costs, too. In April 2006, the U.S. Mint in Denver agreed to pay its female employees almost $9 million to settle claims of sexual harassment. Part of the case was based on raunchy emails. And the mint is not alone. Twenty-seven per cent of Fortune 500 companies have had to address harassment claims involving email.

Advice: If you're looking for a list of what not to joke about on email, look no further than the nondiscrimination policy of your company or an organization you admire. For starters, none of the following is an appropriate launching pad for a comedy routine: race, creed, color, national origin, gender, ethnicity, sexual orientation, religion, marital status, physical disability, or mental illness.

Change the Subject Line

Your Subject line can get you caught up in a legal drag-net if you don't change it every time you move on to a new topic. Let's say you put Company X in your Subject line in January. And let's say, like many of us, you keep that Subject line in place, even though you aren't emailing about Company X anymore. Then let's say Company X gets indicted in April. All your Company X emails—even those that have nothing to do with Company X, even those that have embarrassing details about your personal hygiene problems—are read into the court record. And if you mentioned Company Y, well, it's reeled in, too, as are all the emails that relate to Company Y. So change the Subject line. Please. It's for your own good.

The Email That Shouldn't Have Been Shared

Here's one way a well-intentioned response can lead to trouble. Imagine someone asks you a question via email. You reply that you can't give them an answer because your boss is in Cheshunt. This seemingly innocent bit of information helps the person who wrote to you confirm rumors that the company you work for is about to be bought by Tesco plc. If this person then buys a large amount of stock that attracts government attention, you could wind up in trouble, or at least be swept into an investigation.

Here's another way. A friend sends you the text of a popular book, which he had scanned into his computer. He sends it to your work email and you forward it. Your company is now liable for copyright infringement. (Had he sent it to you at home, you're the only one who would have been guilty and liable, but probably not sued.)

Here's yet another. Your company's attorney sends you an email that's marked "privileged and confidential." You reply and Cc someone outside the firm who has no connection to the case. Congratulations! According to attorneys experienced in this area, if the recipient is not under the umbrella of protection (usually some agency relationship), then privilege is gone, and so is confidentiality. It can now be introduced into court proceedings. And depending on your company policy, that act of forwarding is enough to get you fired—whether the once-privileged email appears in court or not.

And here's one more. In 2006, the U.S. Department of Justice launched an antitrust investigation into at least five major health care companies. As part of the discovery process, one of the companies acknowledged that a contract salesman had sent an email to competitors suggesting a "coordinated response" for the pricing of orthopedic implants to be sold to a hospital. Innocent—albeit stupid—phrase? Or smoking gun? We don't know. What we do know is that it cost the guy his job and that it's costing all these companies a lot of time and money.

Advice: Loose lips sink ships—and so can sharing and forwarding. Also, keep in mind that those increasingly byzantine disclaimers at the bottom of emails you get from your lawyer (and your accountant and your dog groomer) offer only limited protection—no matter how long they are.

Escaping Metadata

All Word documents contain metadata—coding that offers the text's history to anyone savvy enough to mine it. Who sent the original? When did they send it and to whom? Who made changes? All this and possibly more can be discoverable in the hidden or overt coding.

There are lots of examples of sensitive information being accidentally exposed through metadata: military secrets in a report on the death of Italian agent Nicola Calipari in Iraq, disagreements among countries in a United Nations report, strategic advice from partisan operatives in President George W. Bush's supposedly nonpartisan 2005 "National Security Strategy for Victory in Iraq." In each case, the metadata revealed traces of earlier drafts and the names of individuals whose contributions were supposed to have remained hidden.

There are two main sources of this metadata: user profile information and fragments from previous drafts. Users input their names, affiliations, and often their addresses and phone numbers when they start up their computers for the first time, and sometimes again when initially opening applications. This information then automatically attaches itself to just about any document they touch. If you must submit this data (or if your company does it for you), there are a number of ways it can later be removed. It's different with each program. Note that cleaning metadata that reveals previous drafts can be a trickier problem because there are many types of metadata, and most require a different, obscure disabling command. You can always "wash" your files by saving them as text only (Save As>Format: MS-DOS Text), but this will also remove all your formatting. Commercial software programs can rid documents of metadata while still protecting your formatting.

The Email You Should or Shouldn't Have Kept

This is the most contentious and confusing area in email law. What's discoverable in a lawsuit and what isn't? How long do you need to keep email records? Who pays for the enormous cost of recovering emails in a lawsuit? In response to all of this, most firms have formulated a policy for deleting and archiving, and almost every firm's policy is different. The goal is to keep as little as possible but as much as you need to run your business, and that depends on what kind of business you're in.

The fundamental point to keep in mind when archiving is this: be consistent. Keep the same stuff; discard the same stuff. People get into trouble when they deviate and make exceptions. In fact, emails that would have exonerated companies in lawsuits have been thrown out of court because they were not archived according to preexisting policy. Oh, and having a printout doesn't mean you have proof. An email that wasn't harvested off the company's server after papers were served may not hold up in court.

Also, you can't adhere to your company's archival policy retroactively. Look what happened to a partner at Arthur Andersen in the Enron debacle. When things were looking grim, but before records were subpoenaed, this partner took it on himself to engage in an orgy of purging, getting rid of records that could have been deleted earlier under the firm's policy, but hadn't been. The courts did not look kindly on this.

And what do you do if you learn that someone you correspond with is under investigation? According to Elizabeth Charnock, CEO of Cataphora, more people than you might think take this as a cue to race through their inboxes and outboxes, trashing every record of their correspondence with the suspect. Is this wise? Um, no. The investigators probably already have (or will get) a record of your messaging. If you're issued a subpoena, your deletion binge will only make you look guilty.

Finally, remember: the minute your lawyer tells you a subpoena is served, everything freezes. You can't delete any of the relevant emails unless your attorney tells you it's OK to do so. In our litigious society, "freeze letters" are increasingly common. A survey released in 2006 stated that 24 per cent of all employers have been ordered to produce employee email in the course of a lawsuit or regulatory investigation. One U.S. financial firm was recently fined a large sum, in part because the judge ruled that the company had acted in "bad faith" by neglecting to turn over relevant emails. But ineptitude—not just bad faith—can attract a fine and cost you a lawsuit, too.

When lawsuits happen, people immediately worry about everything they wrote. But they also need to worry about emails they received and neglected to answer. Under some statutes, if you are sent an email that alleges wrongdoing or potentially illegal behavior at your firm, you may well need to do something about it.

What should you be looking for? Here's an actual email that was dredged up in a recent case:

> It is all hopeless. It can't be done. We have to let the client know we can't deliver on this contract. There are too many risks and defects.

Did it come from a genuine whistleblower, or from a frayed employee who needed to vent? Who knows? But you have to act on it, whether acting on it means responding to the message, forwarding it to a higher-up, or calling the lawyers.

Advice: Archiving is not an area where there is a lot of room for you to express your individuality or to experiment with different techniques. If you work for a company, follow company policy, be consistent, and don't put your head in the sand.

How to Delete Something
So It Stays Deleted

Some people are hoarders; some are chuckers. Your own behavior should reflect your personal style, within the confines of your company's policy, if it has one. The main thing to consider is that once you do decide to delete, it's like taking the garbage from your kitchen and putting it in your hallway. It's still there. If you really want some piece of email gone, you need to delete it from your inbox, then delete it from your trash, and then employ some further system—a secure delete or a rewriting program—to make sure that it's not just elsewhere on a drive but has in fact been written over sixteen or twenty times and rendered unfindable. That is, you need to take it from your kitchen to your hallway, then from the hallway to the compactor—and then take what comes out of the compactor and throw it into the incinerator. By the way, if you are on a corporate system with proper backup, that probably won't do it. It'll still be there, somewhere. (Unless, of course, the document is one you WANT to find, in which case no one will be able to get it back.)

When in Doubt

So what should you do if you have to communicate information that might be legally sensitive? Well, here's what Eliot Spitzer, New York's governor, had to say on the subject when he was state attorney general: "Never talk when you can nod. And never write when you can talk. My only addendum is never put it in an email."

CHAPTER 7

S.E.N.D.

Now we get to the acronym that gives the book its name. This chapter provides a test—an easy, four-question checklist— to help you determine whether you should or should not hit the Send key.

It's a test we use in our own lives.

At a publishing house and at a newspaper you learn the following: *It's not a mistake if it doesn't wind up in print.* It's the same for email. Nothing bad can happen if you haven't hit the Send key. What you've written can have typos, errors of fact, libelous comments, outright lies, and you know what? It doesn't matter! If you haven't sent it, you still have time to fix it. You can rectify any mistake and nobody will ever know the difference. This is easier said than done, of course. We all have itchy fingers. Send is your computer's most alluring command. But before you succumb, always proofread your document one last time. And while proofreading, keep the following acronym in mind:

S stands for Simple.

E stands for Effective.

N stands for Necessary.

D stands for Done.

If it isn't *simple,* then it will create confusion and waste resources. There's always a value in going over correspondence one last time to see if anything can be stated more clearly. How can you tell whether it's simple enough? Well, start removing words and sentences until the whole thing is as tight and pared down as you can make it without losing your meaning. It's the words that make it past the cut that will determine whether or not your message is effective.

If it isn't *effective,* then try your hardest to make it so. Most correspondence has to get it right the first time out. You may not have another chance to connect with the person you're trying to reach. How do you know your emails are effective? Pay attention to your past mistakes. See if there's anything you can learn from those moments. Maybe even talk to the person for whom your request or message was not effective so that you can correct your error the next time around.

If your email isn't *necessary,* it should be deleted. We all spend far too much time asking one another to do things that are essentially frivolous—and the cost to business and to all of our lives is staggering. If you don't really need to know something, don't ask. The higher you are in an organization, the more important it is to heed this principle. What would happen if you didn't send that email you've just composed? If the answer is "Nothing much," then it's probably best that you trash it. But don't forget: individualized emails that exist solely to reinforce your connection to another person are necessary, too.

Finally, if your email requires action, and you do care whether or not something gets *done* in response, you should, before you hit Send, figure out how you are going to follow up on your email. Just because you asked for it doesn't mean it's going to happen. It's also important to withstand one of email's greatest temptations—that it makes it easy to take the monkey off your back by putting it on someone else's. Is the thing you are asking someone else to do something you should be doing yourself? It's worth remembering that everyone respects the person who takes on the tough jobs, shares the credit, and gets things *done*. It worked this way even before the Information Revolution, and it will continue to work this way no matter what new technologies emerge or where you are in an organization. The final question is really this: "Am I moving things forward, or am I just moving them off my desktop?"

The Last Word

One beautiful winter day, not long ago, David logged on to his computer at the office and found this. Names have been changed, but everything else is exactly as received.

> David,
> I need to know what happened to Rob's piece. Why did it not run? We were clear, you said to me that it was to run the next day or the day after I sent it. This is most unusual that you would solicit a piece from Rob, say that you liked it, told me it would run and then never does.
> Best regards,
> Rob's communications director and spokesperson

To make matters worse, David couldn't remember anything about the piece in question. After fully absorbing the email, he spent the better part of an hour searching his inventory and asking his colleagues whether he had, in fact, accepted an article from Rob and was merely suffering from some form of middle-age memory loss.

When nothing turned up in the search, David felt that he had to address the problem head on, and so he sent an email to Rob's communications director. He apologized if there had been a mix-up but confessed that he had no record of the piece. He asked if Rob would be kind enough to remind him of their discussions and resend the article, along with any initial email correspondence concerning its genesis.

A short while later, David received a curt reply from Rob's communications director. The reason David had not been able to find the piece was that the article had been solicited by and submitted to *another* newspaper's opinion page.

In other words, Rob's communications director had been entirely in the wrong.

What could be more satisfying? Here was a chance for David to write a scorching email. Just think of the possibilities. This is what email is made for, right? There's a trail that proves one's rightness; there's ample time to compose the perfect razor-sharp riposte; there's even the opportunity to Cc several people and maybe Bcc a few others.

And so what did David do? This time around, the better angels of his nature took over, and he sent a "Don't worry about it" email back to Rob's communications director.

We've all had opportunities to rub people's noses in their email errors. But we've also all been in the shoes of Rob's communications director. We've all sent emails where we were hopelessly wrong, or where we were right but got the wrong person, or where we were so self-righteous that no civil discussion could possibly follow.

So here's our plea to everyone who is trying to find his or her way through this new electronic world: Let's all cut one

another *some* slack. Email is too fluid, it's evolving too rapidly, for there to be style police. And etiquette, such as it is, is
situational.

But let's not cut *too* much slack, especially when it comes
to our own behavior. It's within our reach—as senders and
responders—to exercise greater mindfulness and awareness
of what we're doing every single time we send an email. And
when we are more thoughtful and careful with email, it's remarkable the effect that it can have on our lives: fewer people
are mad at us, we get more done, and we can actually look
forward to opening most of the emails we receive.

If you take away only two things from this little book, the
authors sincerely hope it will be these:

Think before you send.

Send email you would like to receive.

APPENDIX

How to Read Your Header

The header of an email contains all the information regarding a message's sender and receiver, its contents, and the path it took to reach you. Most email applications and Webmail systems allow easy viewing of the header.

The annotated header below, for a message from Will's BlackBerry to our friend Dan's account at his university, shows what can be learned from this view. We've created a fictional domain name (.bzz) and, for security reasons, have changed four key numbers and information throughout. Let's take it one clump at a time. We've broken it down into six.

From Will.Schwalbe@dog.bzz Fri Nov 4 14:49:25 2005

This shows the ostensible address and the time on the dog.bzz system when the message was sent.

Return-Path: <Will.Schwalbe@dog.bzz>

This is usually the return address you specify when you configure your email account. It is useful to remember, however, that the return address can be different from the address the mail is sent from. If you're phasing out an email account and transferring to a new one but you still want to send messages from the old account, you can change the return address on that account to your new address. That way, when people respond to you, the reply goes to the new account. Also, many email address books look at the return address to define new contacts. The return path is also displayed in the Reply To field in most messages.

```
Received: from postoffice7.mail.college.edu ([unix socket])
        by postoffice7.mail.college.edu (Cyrus v2.1.11) with
        LMTP; Fri, 04 Nov 2006 14:31:66 -0600
Received: from hermes30.mail.college.edu
        (hermes30.mail.college.edu [132.236.66.66]) by
        postoffice7.mail.college.edu (8.12.10/8.12.6) with
        ESMTP idjA4JVnMc016663 for
        <djg46@postoffice7.mail.college.edu>; Fri, 4 Nov 2006
        14:31:49 -0600 (EST)
Received: from filter01.mail.college.edu
        (filter01.mail.college.edu [132.236.66.31]) by
        hermes30.mail.college.edu (8.12.10/8.12.6) with
        ESMTP id jA4JVklu021636 for
        <djg46@postoffice7.mail.college.edu>; Fri, 4 Nov 2006
        14:31:47 -0600 (EST)
Received: (from daemon@localhost) by
        filter01.mail.college.edu (8.12.10/8.12.6) id
        jA4JVkND022994 for
        djg46@postoffice7.mail.college.edu; Fri, 4 Nov 2006
```

14:31:46 -0600 (EST)

Received: from mail12.newcom.bzz (mail12.newcom.bzz
[192.196.66.30]) by filter01.mail.college.edu
(8.12.10/8.12.6) with ESMTP id jA4JVfob022826 for
<djg46@college.edu>; Fri, 4 Nov 2006 14:31:41 -0600
(EST)

Received: from imr11.newcom.pvt (imr11.newcom.pvt
[163.6.60.111]) by mail12.newcom.bzz with ESMTP; Fri,
4 Nov 2006 14:31:40 -0600

Received: from sm-AZPH-xc03.wdw.newcom.bzz (sm-
AZPH-xc03.wdw.newcom.bzz [172.16.177.30]) by
imr11.newcom.pvt with ESMTP; Fri, 4 Nov 2006
14:31:39 -0600

Received: from SM-AZPH-XC02.wdw.newcom.bzz
([172.16.177.19]) by sm-AZPH-xc03.wdw.newcom.bzz
with Microsoft SMTPSVC (6.0.2196.6713); Fri, 4 Nov
2006 14:31:39 -0600

Received: from sm-nyny-xc04.nena.wdpr.newcom.bzz
([167.13.137.86]) by SM-AZPH-XC02.wdw.newcom.bzz
with Microsoft SMTPSVC (6.0.2196.6713); Fri, 4 Nov
2006 14:31:38 -0600

Received: from sm-nyny-xm06.nena.wdpr.newcom.bzz
([167.13.137.80]) by sm-nyny-
xc04.nena.wdpr.newcom.bzz with Microsoft SMTPSVC
(6.0.2196.6713); Fri, 4 Nov 2006 14:31:37 -0600

This part of the header shows the path the message took
across the network. The list tracks the message backward starting from the receiver's mail system. Presumably, Will's Black-
Berry sends the message via a telecom company's wireless
system, which is invisibly connected to a BlackBerry server at

the pseudonymous parent company, Newcom. Naming conventions can be deduced from patterns in the header. We would guess that this message originated at a mail server for Newcom's Northeast North America division in New York City and traveled via Phoenix, Arizona. Next it went to a "private" (.pvt, i.e., local) mail server somewhere, and then to another Newcom server, which sent the message to the university system.

After passing through a number of "filter" mail servers (for weeding out spam), the message is delivered to Dan's mail allocation. The trip took thirty-one seconds. Of course, if the Newcom clock and the university clock were not in sync, this travel time might not be accurate. Also, note that delivery simply means that the receiver's mail server has the file, not that it has been looked at or downloaded by the user.

```
X-MimeOLE: Produced By Microsoft Exchange V6.0.6606.0
content-class: urn:content-classes:message
MIME-Version: 1.0
Content-Type: multipart/alternative;
     boundary="——_=_NextPart_001_01C6E176.6F8640B6"
```

The above indicates that the message has been formatted in MIME (Multipurpose Internet Mail Extensions) format. MIME handles symbols and numbers, characters that are not standard characters, and attachments. In this case, the mixed character formats (from Will's BlackBerry and Dan's Mac, presumably) in the message caused the system to divide the message into two parts, requiring MIME. The header gives details about those parts. It also shows, in the top line above, that the server that actually sent the message passed through Microsoft Exchange, which uses a proprietary format to communicate between clients and the server.

```
Subject: Re: NYC and CBGB
Date: Fri, 4 Nov 2006 14:31:37 -0600
Message-Id:
    <1F9C633C4C481B4BB93E96A13DF670C0071301A8
    @sm-nynyxm06.nena.wdpr.newcom.bzz>
```

The Message-Id is a unique identifier that your mail server assigns to each message it transmits. This allows you to retrieve that message from the server even when copies of it have been modified or destroyed on your computer's email client. (See POP vs. IMAP, pages 31–2).

```
X-MS-Has-Attach:
X-MS-TNEF-Correlator:
Thread-Topic: NYC and CBGB
Thread-Index:
    AcXhc6EqGyOQWJbiTPOWbqnqa3NLrQAAs+06
X-PH: V4.1@filter01
From: "Schwalbe, Will" <Will.Schwalbe@dog.bzz>
To: <djg46@college.edu>
X-OriginalArrivalTime: 04 Nov 2006 19:31:37.0906 (UTC)
    FILETIME=[6FC4F120:01C6E176]
X-PMX-Version: 4.7.1.128076, Antispam-Engine: 2.1.0.0,
    Antispam-Data: 2006.11.4.20
X-PMX-Version: 4.7.1.128076, Antispam-Engine: 2.0.3.0,
    Antispam-Data: 2006.11.4.20
```

This part shows information about spam filters through which the message passed. It also shows the semiofficial arrival time, though in this case it refers to the moment when the message left the Microsoft server on Will's end.

Given that emails are chopped into packets and these are sent across the network on potentially thousands of different paths to their destination, you may wonder how the path listed in the header is determined. It turns out that the header only lists the servers that the message passed through, not each individual router and switch along the journey. Servers are "real" computers, whereas routers and switches are essentially just fancy modems. The servers that transmit a message to its destination tend to be the same for each packet, which is listed in the header. The ubiquity and invisibility of intermediate routers and switches—which each save information about all recent transmissions—is one reason privacy advocates caution against sending sensitive material by email.

ACKNOWLEDGMENTS

The authors would like jointly to acknowledge:

Marty Asher, who believed in this book and us from the second he heard about it. He is the editor's editor, and his contributions to *Send* are immense. Deep thanks, too, to Sonny Mehta, Tony Chirico, Pat Johnson, Paul Bogaards, Katherine Hourigan, Farah Miller, Carol Janeway, Nicholas Latimer, Peter Mendelsund, Jon Segal, Zachary Wagman, Arianna Cassidy, Margaux Wexberg-Sanchez, Virginia Tan, Victoria Pearson, Marci Lewis, Erinn Hartman, Gabrielle Brooks, and all the other amazing people at Knopf.

We were also incredibly lucky to find in Canongate an equally passionate and inspired publisher. We are tremendously grateful to Jamie Byng, Anya Serota, Jenny Todd, Dan Franklin, Helen Bleck and the rest of the remarkable team.

John Brockman, Katinka Matson, and Max Brockman are great agents and even better friends. They have been instrumental at every stage. Thanks also to Michael Healey and Russell Weinberger.

We were very fortunate to find Daniel Graham, a superb researcher with vast stores of knowledge, endless curiosity, and eclectic interests. His work has been invaluable, as was Nora

Salvatore's legal research. Alice Truax helped us in so many ways as we prepared the manuscript. We thank her for her challenging questions and eagle eye. Thanks also to Elizabeth Pearson-Griffiths.

This book would not exist without the extraordinary Andrew Brimmer, Tom Molner, and Naomi Wolf. We are more grateful to them than we can say. Marco Pasanella and Rebecca Robertson were the source of constant verbal and liquid cheer. Josef Astor, brilliant photographer and great pal, moved mountains.

And for generously offering advice, help, and sharing research: Chris Anderson, Joel Ariaratnam, Larry Ashmead, Albert-László Barabási, Naomi S. Baron, Jude Biersdorfer, Paul Bloom, Carmine Boccusi, Rob Brodsky, Bruce Brothers, Andrew Carroll, Elizabeth Charnock and Rick Janowski of Cataphora, Alison Clarkson, Christine Finn, Bill Fitzsimmons, Steve Goldstein, Dan Goleman, Judith Harris, Leslie Koch, Kris Kliemann, Patrick Lencioni, Randy Lipsitz, Margret McBride, Nicholas McGegan, Robin Mamlet, Marion Maneker, David Myers, Betsy Perry, V. S. Ramachandran, Kit Reed, Mark Reiter, Richard Rothschild, Ben Schott, Elena Seibert, Steve Strogatz, Deborah Tannen, Calvin Trillin, Yossi Vardi, Suzy Welch, Carol Weston, and Kim Yorio.

Will Schwalbe would also like to thank for their help:
Bill Adler, Ellen Archer, Sherry Arden, Quang Bao, Sarah Barnum, Kedron Barrett, Carl Bazil, Marjory Berkowitz, Michael Bilavsky, Ann Bramson, Darrell Brown, Mike Bryant, Roger Canevari, Mark Chait, Art Chang, Jay Corcoran, Lisa Cortes, D. C. Cymbalista, Brian DeFiore, Florence DeVecchi,

Acknowledgments

Vincent Dixon, Ed Douglas, Lisa Drew, Elisabeth and David Kallick Dyssegaard, Bob and Sally Edgar, Valja Engelhardt, Maia Ettinger, Ed Finn, Virginia Fowler, Molly O'Neil Frank, Eric Garber, Mr. Gill, Harvey Ginsberg, Nikki Giovanni, Sally Girvin, Chris and Siuli GoGwilt, Emily Gould, Linda Greenlaw, Maria Guarnaschelli, David and Jean Halberstam, Nathan Haratz, Peter Hedges, Cheryl Henson, Larry Hughes, Jeff Hunter, Amy Jedlicka, David Kaiser, Walter Kaiser, David Kissinger, Larry Kramer, Doug Lee, Martha Levin, Phyllis Levin, Nancy Lorenz, Laurinda Lowenstein, Rodger McFarlane, John McGlynn, Nina McPherson, Al Marchioni, Bob Miller, Fiona Moore, Amalie Moses, Herb Nagourney, Leslie Norton, Mary Ellen O'Neill, Señor Ordóñez, Regina Peruggi, Ben Pesner, Eric Price, Lisa Queen, Joseph Rabatin, Gerard Raymond, Bill Reichblum, Ricardo Restrepo, Lee Rich, Jean Guy Roberge, Michael Roberts, Alex Rockwell, Ainlay Samuels, John Samuels III, Zach Schisgal, Lee Schrager, Douglas Schwalbe, Mary Anne Schwalbe, Douglas J. Schwalbe, Nina Schwalbe, Fabienne Schwalbe, Pippa Scott, Jeff Seroy, Ken Shimonishi, Jeff Slonim, Barbara Spence, Alan Staschke, Doug Stumpf, Allison Thrush, George Tracy, Peternelle Van Arsdale, Ed Victor, Claire Wachtel, Ted Washburn, David Webster, Will Winkelstein. Also nephews Nicolas, Adrian, Milo, and Cy Schwalbe, and niece Lucy Schwalbe; as well as godchildren Swift Edgar, Ilya Barrett, Ming Lee, and Sophie Kissinger.

And David Cheng, for all and more.

David Shipley would like to thank:
Todd Alden, Franscis Balken, Kaleigh Balken, Nancy Bekavac, Andrew Bell, Fred Buchwalter, Marianne Buchwalter, John

Cestar, John Collier, Gail Collins, Sam Crawley, Benjamin Dean, Owen Shipley Dean, Mary Duenwald, Jim Duffy, Susan Ellingwood, Eric Etheridge, Tom Freedman, James Gibney, Toby Harshaw, Arthur Hertzberg, George Hodgman, George Kalogerakis, Lyubov Kozelko, Emmy Kulshreshtha, Dorothy Lesman, Max Lesman, Lawrence Levi, Mike Levitas, Joseph V. Long III, Mark Lotto, Carmel McCoubrey, Salvatore Macri, Gloria Marrero, Alice Mayhew, Adam Moss, Peter Muz, Lawrence Raab, Brian Rea, Katy Roberts, Andy Rosenthal, Jack Rosenthal, Ingrid Rosner, Laura Secor, Herbert Semler, Shirley Semler, Jania Shevchenko, Ann Shipley, Erna Shipley, Fiona Sullivan Shipley, Joan Shipley, John Shipley, Joseph Shipley, Julian Shipley, Katherine Shipley, Rosa Shipley, Thomas Shipley, Andrew Sullivan, Megan Sullivan, Rosario Vasconez, Sam Weber, Frank Wilkinson, Inell Willis, Deborah Wolf, Leonard Wolf. And M. V. Riddell, for everything.

NOTES

Introduction: Why Do We Email So Badly?

1 **Jo Moore's emails:** Reproduced on the *Guardian*'s website.

5 **Bob Geldof:** Quoted by Martin Shankleman, on *www.BBC.co.uk*, November 15, 2005.

6 **Office workers spend:** 2003 survey released by the American Management Association and the ePolicy Institute.

6 **In 2009, the Bush administration:** Alan Weinstein, archivist of the United States, from "From the Archivist to You" on *www.archives .gov*, January 17, 2006.

7 **As linguist Naomi Baron has noted:** Naomi Baron, *Alphabet to Email: How Written English Evolved and Where It's Heading* (New York: Routledge, 2000), pp. 216ff.

9 **As Daniel Goleman told us:** Author interview with Daniel Goleman.

Chapter 1: When Should We Email?

13 **Fashion store email:** *New York Times,* August 8, 2006.

13 **Radio Shack email:** *New York Times,* August 31, 2006.

16 **Bill Gates on voicemail:** Bill Gates, "The Unified Communications Revolution," on *www.microsoft.com,* June 26, 2006.

16 **Duncan Watts research:** Peter S. Dodds, Roby Muhamad, and Duncan J. Watts, "An Experimental Study of Search in Global Social Net-

works," *Science* 301 (2003): 827–29.

18 **In the early 1960s:** James Gillies and Robert Cailliau, *How the Web Was Born* (Oxford: Oxford University Press, 2000), pp. 11–25, 44, 78–79. Stephen Segaller, *NERDS 2.0.1: A Brief History of the Internet* (New York: TV Books, 1998). Barry M. Leiner, Vinton G. Cerf, David D. Clark, Robert E. Kahn, Leonard E. Kleinrock, Daniel C. Lynch, Jon Postel, Larry G. Roberts, and Stephen Wolff, "A Brief History of the Internet," The Internet Society (2003), *www.isoc.org/internet/history/brief.shtml,* accessed on July 12, 2006.

18 **The world's first email:** Ray Tomlinson, "The First Network Email," *openmap.bbn.com/~tomlinso/ray/firstemailframe.html,* accessed on July 12, 2006.

19 **Initially, ARPANET's physical network:** Leonard Kleinrock, *Queueing Systems,* Vol. 2 (New York: Wiley-Interscience, 1976), p. 306.

19 **Once the rules were in place:** MCI Mail. Katie Hafner, "Billions Served Daily, and Counting," *The New York Times,* December 6, 2001.

22 **David Haig, a head tutor:** Email from David Haig to authors.

22 **"Ever since email came on the scene":** Author interview with William R. Fitzsimmons.

23 **Here's what Bill Gates does:** Bill Gates, "How I Work," *Fortune,* April 7, 2006.

24 **As Clive Thompson pointed out:** Clive Thompson, "Meet the Life Hackers," *New York Times Magazine,* October 16, 2005.

26 **Abramoff emails:** Philip Shenon, "In Messages, Lobbyist Says DeLay Pressed for Donations," *New York Times,* December 15, 2005.

27 **"The real scandal here is":** Quoted by Tom Hamburger, "Nonpartisan Testimony Gets White House Edit," *Los Angeles Times,* May 19, 2005.

28 **Harlan Coben and Richard Dooling emails:** Courtesy of Coben and Dooling.

28 **People are forgiving:** Keith Rayner, Sarah J. White, Rebecca L. Johnson, and Simon P. Liversedge, "Raeding Wrods With Jumbled Lettres," *Psychological Science* 17 (2006): 192–93.

30 **The Internet is the network of nodes:** Ed Krol, *The Whole Internet User's Guide and Catalog* (Sebastopol, Calif.: O'Reilly & Associates, 1992).

31 **Simple Mail Transfer Protocol, or SMTP:** "Simple Mail Transfer Protocol," *Wikipedia* (2006), *en.wikipedia.org/wiki/Simple_Mail_ Transfer_Protocol,* accessed on July 14, 2006.

31 **Multipurpose Internet Mail Extensions, or MIME:** "Multipurpose Internet Mail Extensions," *Wikipedia* (2006), *en.wikipedia.org/wiki/ MIME,* accessed on July 14, 2006.

31 **For most of us:** "Managing e-mail is an increasing burden," *Financial Times,* July 12, 2006, Digital Business supplement, p. 5, U.S. ed.

31 **POP (Post Office Protocol) and IMAP:** "Internet Message Access Protocol," *Wikipedia* (2006), *en.wikipedia.org/wiki/Internet_ Message_Access_Protocol,* accessed on July 14, 2006.

32 **In a 2006 study, 1,400 office workers:** Digital Etiquette survey conducted for Telewest Business by TNS, reported in "Do You Know Your Netiquette?" *Manchester Evening News,* online edition, March 13, 2006.

34 **As Tom Wheeler writes:** Tom Wheeler, *Mr. Lincoln's T-Mails: The Untold Story of How Abraham Lincoln Used the Telegraph to Win the Civil War* (New York: Collins, 2006), p. 183.

35 **Even pioneering Hewlett-Packard:** Robert Johnson, "The Fax Machine: Technology That Refuses to Die," *New York Times,* March 27, 2005.

37 **Robin Mamlet, former dean of admissions:** Author interview with Robin Mamlet.

41 **According to the most recent:** Eulynn Shiu and Amanda Lenhart, "How Americans use instant messaging," *Pew Internet and American Life Project* survey, September 1, 2004.

42 **Kit Reed, a professor of English:** Author interview with Kit Reed, and as quoted by Kara Maguire, "Anonymous Writing Students Attend Class on Line," the Wesleyan *Argus,* 2002.

45 **"We simultaneously look forward":** Author interview with Naomi S. Baron.

46 **But the reliability also comes from:** Stephen Segaller, *NERDS 2.0.1: A Brief History of the Internet* (New York: TV Books, 1998), pp. 110–13.

46 **This is accomplished by having:** Help with this section was provided by Dan Sheldon (Department of Computer Science, Cornell University).

46   **In 2005, MIT researchers:** Mike Afergan and Robert Beverly, "The State of the Email Address," *ACM SIGCOMM Computer Communications Review* 35 (2005): 29–35. This reference was provided by Dan Sheldon (Department of Computer Science, Cornell University).

Chapter 2: The Anatomy of an Email

54   **Patrick Lencioni, the author:** Author interview with Patrick Lencioni.

58   **In the middle of a computer training session:** Simone Sebastian, "Law School Admissions Chief Misfires on E-mail," *San Francisco Chronicle,* February 22, 2006.

80   **How CAN You Tell:** Jane Spencer, "Shirk Ethic: How to Fake a Hard Day at the Office," *Wall Street Journal,* May 15, 2003.

86   **.gif: another image format:** "GIF," *Wikipedia* (2006), *en.wikipedia .org/wiki/GIF,* accessed on July 28, 2006.

91   **In a recent survey, many employers:** Study of three thousand email users by i.Tech Dynamic, cited by Iain Thompson, "This Is Very Annoying," *www.vnunet.com,* July 29, 2005.

95   **Lord Nelson, in his letters:** *The Dispatches and Letters of Lord Nelson,* Nicolas Edition (London: Chatham, 1997; originally published in 1845).

95   **When Jack Kerouac began a letter:** March 1943 letter to Sebastian Sampas, quoted in *Letters of a Nation,* ed. Andrew Carroll (New York: Kondansha, 1997), p. 308.

97   **How to Say @ in Many Languages:** From *www.herodios.com,* featured in Steve Bass's Tips & Tweaks column, *www.pcworld.com,* November 2, 2005. Additional research by Søren Dyssegaard.

100 **George Soros's institute:** Author interviews with employees.

104 **Scientists have discovered cells in the brain:** Giacomo Rizzolatti, Luciano Fadiga, Vittorio Gallese, and Leonardo Fogassi, "Premotor Cortex and the Recognition of Motor Actions," *Cognitive Brain Research* 3 (1996): 131–41.

104 **Michael Arbib, a computer scientist:** Michael A. Arbib, "From Monkey-like Action Recognition to Human Language: An Evolutionary Framework for Neurolinguistics," *Behavioral and Brain Sciences* 28 (2005): 105–67.

104 **An experiment conducted by the French psychologist:** Nicolas Guéguen, "Help on the Web: The Effect of the Same First Name Between the Sender and the Receptor in a Request Made by Email," *Psychological Record* 53 (2003): 459–66.

106 **Wilde letter:** Letter to Robert Ross, June 3, 1897, quoted in *The Complete Letters of Oscar Wilde,* ed. Merlin Holland and Rupert Hart-Davis (New York: Holt, 2000), p. 877.

108 **Tony Wheeler, the founder:** Email to author from Tony Wheeler.

Chapter 3: How to Write (the Perfect) Email

113 **Ming Lee on emailing:** Reprinted by permission of Ming Lee.

117 **The senior management there is fond of cow jokes:** See *www.stonyfield.com,* accessed on Aug 20, 2006.

117 **Sean White on winning a gold medal:** Quoted by Gavin Edwards, "Attack of the Flying Tomato," *Rolling Stone,* March 9, 2006.

119 **Kennedy memos:** *JFK Wants to Know: Memos from the President's Office, 1961–1963,* ed. Edward B. Claflin (New York: William Morrow, 1991), pp. 59, 141, 242.

127 **A study of email users:** Study of three thousand email users by i.Tech Dynamic, cited by Iain Thompson, "This Is Very Annoying," *www.vnunet.com,* July 29, 2005.

128 **You can program your computer to turn Caps Lock off:** See *www.wired.com/news/technology/0,71606-0.html* and *www.worldstart.com/tips/shared/capslocktrick.htm* and *blogs.pcworld.com/tipsandtweaks/archives/002427.html,* all accessed November 12, 2006.

132 **Susan Farren's email:** Reprinted by permission of Sue Farren, author of *The Fireman's Wife* (New York: Hyperion, 2005).

133 **Tellingly, researchers at Cornell:** Jeffrey T. Hancock, Lauren E. Curry, Saurabh Goorha, & Michael T. Woodworth, "Lies in Conversation: An Examination of Deception Using Automated Linguistic Analysis," *Proceedings, Annual Conference of the Cognitive Science Society* 26 (2004): 534–540.

133 **James Dilworth's appeal:** Reprinted by permission of James Dilworth, CEO of Real Life Gifts.

Chapter 4: The Six Essential Types of Email

136 **Email to Carol Weston:** Author interview with Carol Weston.

137 **A study at Stanford in 1990:** Elizabeth Newton, "Overconfidence in the Communication of Intent: Heard and Unheard Melodies," Ph.D. dissertation, Stanford University, Palo Alto, Calif. (1990), cited in Justin Kruger, Nicholas Epley, Jason Parker, and Zhi-Wen Ng, "Egocentrism Over E-Mail: Can We Communicate as Well as We Think?" *Journal of Personality and Social Psychology* 89 (2005): 925–36.

140 **When making a large request:** Jonathan L. Freedman and Scott C. Fraser, "Compliance Without Pressure: The Foot-in-the-Door Technique," *Journal of Personality and Social Psychology* 4 (1966): 195–202. This study was brought to our attention by James Cutting (Department of Psychology, Cornell University).

141 **Nicolas Guéguen, the French researcher:** Nicolas Guéguen, "Foot-in-the-Door Technique and Computer-Mediated Communication," *Computers in Human Behavior* 18 (2002): 11–15.

144 **This Is Annoying How:** Adapted from a post by Rob DeWitt on July 15, 2006, on Steve Bass's Tips & Tweaks at *blogs.pcworld.com/tipsandtweaks/archives/002408.html.*

144 **There's more than one way to be polite:** Penelope Brown and Stephen C. Levinson, *Politeness: Some Universals in Language Usage* (Cambridge, United Kingdom: Cambridge University Press, 1978), pp. 17–21.

145 **Alison Clarkson's suggestions:** Author interview with Alison Clarkson.

147 **Researchers have shown that providing an out:** Nicolas Guéguen and Alexandra Pascual, "Improving the Response Rate to a Street Survey: An Evaluation of the 'But You are Free to Accept or Refuse' Technique," *The Psychological Record* 55 (2005): 297–303.

148 **Emily's email:** Used by permission of Emily Queen.

149 **A 2006 survey asked office workers:** Digital Etiquette survey conducted for Telewest Business by TNS, reported in "Do You Know Your Netiquette" *Manchester Evening News,* online edition, March 13, 2006.

151 **Jack Welch, the former head of General Electric:** Author interview with Suzy Welch.

153 **Barabási came to this conclusion:** Albert-László Barabási, "Darwin and Einstein Correspondence Patterns," *Science* 437 (2005): 1251.

156 **try re-sorting your inbox:** See also tips at *www.blueflavor.com/ ed/tips_tricks/get_control_of_your_inbox.php*, accessed on December 4, 2006.

156 **(Soon your computer may be able):** Thanks to Dan Sheldon (Department of Computer Science, Cornell University).

157 **Here is the last-ditch strategy:** Lawrence Lessig, *Wired,* August 2006.

160 **Suzy Welch, the business writer:** Author interview with Suzy Welch.

Chapter 5: The Emotional Email

169 **Abdala-Korman exchange:** As posted on February 19, 2006, on *abcnews.go.com/Nightline/story?id=1635684,* and on February 15, 2006, on *www.masslawyersweekly.com/break021506.cfm.*

171 **In a study conducted by:** Dan Gilbert, "He Who Casts the First Stone Probably Didn't," Op-Ed page, *New York Times,* July 24, 2006.

176 **Loeb-Lewis exchange:** London *Financial Times,* April 1, 2005. Also as posted on April 15, 2005, on *news.wallstreetandtech.efinancial careers.com/ITEM_FR/newsItemId-3884.*

176 **Larry Kramer, writer and activist:** Email to author from Larry Kramer.

177 **As the linguist Deborah Tannen:** Author interview with Deborah Tannen. See also Deborah Tannen, *The Argument Culture: Stopping America's War of Words* (New York: Random House, 1998).

179 **And yet people rarely suspect:** Justin Kruger, Nicholas Epley, Jason Parker, and Zhi-Wen Ng, "Egocentrism Over E-Mail: Can We Communicate as Well as We Think?" *Journal of Personality and Social Psychology* 89 (2005): 925–36. This study was brought to our attention by Dennis Regan (Department of Psychology, Cornell University.)

185 **In case you were worried:** Debunking courtesy of Mark Liberman, *Language Log* (2005), *http://itre.cis.upenn.edu/~myl/languagelog/ archives/002493.html,* accessed on December 3, 2005. Typical misleading news report about this study: Robert Stansfield, "Txting Mks U Stpid," *Daily Mirror* (United Kingdom), April 22, 2005.

186 **Richard Phillips, a London lawyer:** Katie Fraser, *The Express,*

September 29, 2005.

188 **Some email providers have found a way:** Rob Scher, "How to 'Unsend' E-mail Sent in Error," *Smart Computing* 12 (2001): 89–91.

189 **If you happen to be using Outlook:** Daniel Graham interview. See also *office.microsoft.com/en-us/outlook/HA010917601033.aspx*, accessed on December 3, 2006.

Chapter 6: The Email That Can Land You in Jail

190 **William Morris firings:** *Daily Variety,* April 28, 1992.

191 **Think Merck, where the discovery:** J. Bonasia, "Awash in E-mail, Firms Embrace E-Discovery," *Investor's Business Daily,* January 31, 2006.

191 **Not surprisingly, the electronic discovery business is booming:** Estimates by InfoTrends/Cap Ventures and Socha-Gelbman, quoted in "Oce Business Services to Acquire CaseData Inc., E-Discovery and Litigation Support Pioneer," *PR Newswire,* October 6, 2006.

191 **Employee email:** Judy Mann, "A Little Vanity, A Lot of Corporate Greed: A Killer Combo," *Washington Post,* June 6, 2001.

192 **A company called Cataphora:** Author interview with Elizabeth Charnock, CEO of Cataphora, Inc.

194 **"I am very uncomfortable with":** Quote provided by Cataphora, Inc.

199 **These findings are borne out in other ways:** Roger Matus and Sean True, "Monsters in Your Mailbox," InBoxer, Inc., study (2005), *www.inboxer.com/downloads/Monsters_In_Your_Mailbox.pdf*, accessed October 20, 2006.

199 **In April 2006, the U.S. Mint:** Anne C. Mulkern, "Mint Chief: No Tolerance for Sexual Harassment," *Denver Post,* September 15, 2006.

199 **Twenty-seven per cent of Fortune 500 companies:** According to a 2000 Assurex eRisk study conducted by the Human Resource Institute of Eckerd College, Florida, as cited at *www.epolicyinstitute .com/press/einsurance.html.*

201 **In 2006, the U.S. Department of Justice:** Lisa Urquhart, "S&N Salesman in US Anti-Trust Probe," *Financial Times,* August 1, 2006.

202 **There are lots of examples:** "Content Security in the News,"

Metadatarisk.org, *www.metadatarisk.org/news/news_overview.htm*, accessed on July 20, 2006.

203   **Cleaning metadata that reveals previous drafts:** "How to Minimize Metadata in Word 2003," Microsoft Corp., *support.microsoft.com/kb/825576*, accessed on July 20, 2006.

204   **Look what happened to a partner at Arthur Andersen:** Kurt Eichenwald, "Ex-Accounting Chief at Enron is Indicted on Six Felony Charges," *New York Times,* January 23, 2004.

204   **According to Elizabeth Charnock:** Author interview with Elizabeth Charnock, CEO of Cataphora, Inc.

205   **A survey released in 2006:** 2006 Workplace E-mail, Instant Messaging & Blog Survey by the American Management Association and the ePolicy Institute.

205   **One U.S. financial firm was recently fined $1.45 billion:** Landon Thomas, Jr., *New York Times,* May 19, 2005.

205   **It is all hopeless:** Email provided by Cataphora, Inc.

207   **Spitzer quote:** Eliot Spitzer, "Cleaning Up Capitalism," *Fast Company,* January 1, 1995.

Appendix: How to Read Your Header

214   **The header of an email:** Help with this section was provided by Dan Sheldon (Department of Computer Science, Cornell University); interview with Dan Graham in Ithaca, New York, July 19, 2006.

215   **If you're phasing out an email account:** This tip came from Lou Dolinar, "Forwarding and multiple mailboxes manage home and office conflicts," *Lou's Day* (2006), *www.dolinar.com.*

INDEX